Tales of the
'Truly Unpleasant

Tales of the Truly Unpleasant

Humor columns by
Steve Johnston

iUniverse, Inc.
New York   Bloomington

Tales of the Truly Unpleasant

iUniverse books may be ordered through booksellers or by contacting:

iUniverse
1663 Liberty Drive
Bloomington, IN 47403
www.iuniverse.com
1-800-Authors (1-800-288-4677)

Because of the dynamic nature of the Internet, any Web addresses or links contained in
this book may have changed since publication and may no longer be valid. The views
expressed in this work are solely those of the author and do not necessarily reflect the
views of the publisher, and the publisher hereby disclaims any responsibility for them.

ISBN: 978-1-4502-2204-4 (sc)
ISBN: 978-1-4502-2205-1 (dj)
ISBN: 978-1-4502-2206-8 (ebook)

Printed in the United States of America

iUniverse rev. date: 04/22/2010

Table of Contents

Foreword

By Molly Johnston

My dad, Steve Johnston, wrote something like 300 "Sunday Punch" columns for The Seattle Times, sharing potentially embarrassing details of our everyday lives as a family – or at least his version of our lives. So what was it like to be one of his kids, never knowing what he might be writing?

I can speak for myself, as the youngest of the four Johnston kids. Every Monday, while I wandered through the halls of my school or picked my desk in a class, I would get comments from various teachers about how great my dad's article was the previous day. These comments went on for all my middle school and high school career. I'd obviously try to utilize them to my benefit, and increase whatever grade I was already receiving in class.

But of course, being the slacker teenager that I was, I couldn't have cared less about what story my dad wrote up in the weekend's Sunday Punch. When a teacher would mention it, I would smile and nod and pretend like I knew what they were talking about. Granted, I normally would since it was always the latest event in the Johnston household.

But I didn't really start reading, and appreciating, the articles until I began to put this book together. Now, I have thoroughly enjoyed the silly stories that my dad shared with the greater Seattle area. I'm even more grateful that we have them recorded and will be able to share these with all the future Johnston generations!

I would get in big trouble from my big brothers if I tried to speak on their behalf, so I decided to give them a chance. Here they are, from the next one older than me up to the oldest:

> **Barrett:** My dad has that special talent of being able both to embarrass and thoroughly entertain his children, usually at the same time. What son could forget standing in the middle of the street swinging at

a baseball tied to a stick with fishing line, or wandering around on the stilts Dad had made for us – all this while neighbors drove by, looking at us oddly? Meanwhile, his columns brought some small level of celebrity among our social group, who constantly quizzed us about our exploits or about the true nature of our mother.

As for our home life – after about the 300th time of hearing, "When I was a kid in Everett...," we all just rolled our eyes and chuckled about whatever semi-true story it was we were on the verge of hearing.

Tim: Growing up I always knew that anything I did could end up in a Sunday Punch. I remember one time my dad made the mistake of baking a cake when I had a couple of friends over. He had just taken it out of the oven and it wasn't long before the smell brought us boys to the kitchen.

We thought it would be a good idea to go ahead and eat as much cake as we could fit in our mouths (being teenagers, this wasn't a hard task). Of course my dad came back right as we were finishing up and started questioning us. A few weeks later one of my friends brought in a copy of the Sunday Punch and, not surprisingly, my dad had written about our cake feast. Even less surprisingly, he had made the story sound much funnier than it seemed at the time. My friend was bragging and showing everyone at school, but to me it was just another day in the life as one of the children of Steve "I can make a funny story out of anything" Johnston.

Eric: "Your last name is Johnston? Are you related to Steve Johnston? We love the Sunday Punch!" There were numerous instances like that, when my last name got me some superstar status. While we were growing up, my friends' parents would always tell me how funny his stories were.

Sunday mornings, I would open Pacific and look for the Sunday Punch. There would be times I would have a good laugh – and other times when I would read the story and say to my wife, "Wow, Dad really took some writer's privilege with *that* story!" But all in all, I am very proud of my father and all those stories – even with some of their "extras." And thanks to my sister Molly for putting this together!

Well, that's the word from the Johnston children. But what about the "Truly Unpleasant Mrs. Johnston"? In her own defense, my mom says that while her husband's columns are amusing, they are not to be taken literally. She points out, for example, that many of her friends don't think she is unpleasant. "Most people think I am fairly nice," she says. And I wholeheartedly agree with them.

Acknowledgements

There are a number of people I want to thank, on behalf of my dad and family, for their help in putting this book together.

A special thank you to the two artists who offered to create brand-new illustrations for the book, Fred Birchman and Paul Schmid. This book would not be complete without the sort of cartoons that went along with the Sunday Punch for more than 20 years! My dad always enjoyed that neither of you drew a true representation of what he looked like, and that you pulled these images out of the imaginations of two unique artists. Thank you very much for your help and support in this project (and Fred, thanks also for helping with the photos and layout questions).

S.L. Sanger, thank you for the help in finding a publisher that would be most beneficial for this book.

Kathy Triesch for helping to get this book moving along and setting me up with the right people to connect with. And without you these stories wouldn't exist: thank you for introducing my parents to one another!

Jackie Broom, my dad's "very, very, very best friend in the whole world," thank you for your support through this time and making my dad laugh.

Thanks to all the people at The Seattle Times who helped look through the archives and arrange for permission to reprint some of this work.

Most importantly, an enormous thank you to Bill Ristow. Without his involvement, this book would have taken years to complete and would not be the caliber it is today. I'll never be able to express my full appreciation for all of the time and effort you have put in to help create this book! I know my dad and the rest of the family truly appreciate all of your hard work. Thank you, thank you, thank you!

And finally, a thank you to my mom and dad. Mom, for allowing Dad to write all of these crazy stories throughout the years, and putting up with his "extensions of the truth." Dad, thank you for finding your passion and sticking with it. As well as documenting our childhood and sharing the way you saw things.

– Molly Johnston

Preface

By Steve Johnston

I guess I have been writing funny things about as long as I can remember.

Once in the 7th grade, I wrote a "love note" from the prettiest girl in the 7th grade to the geekiest kid, and the teacher intercepted the note and called my mother. The teacher told my mother about the love note but he was laughing so hard that he could barely explain the note.

As a punishment the teacher made me write a paper on why not to pass notes in class. Of course, I made the paper humorous.

But I didn't know I could make money writing this kind of thing until I got into junior college. The paper was paying $10 per column and I started writing humor columns about college life. This continued from Everett Community College until I went to Western Washington University, where I started writing a column called "On the Home Front." It came out twice a week and paid $25 each time.

I invented a student named Irving Bingo. Irving was a typical slack-jawed, lazy student. His whole goal was to avoid going to class, drinking coffee in the student lounge instead. He also made fun of all the professors. I remember one teacher said he dreaded seeing me sign up for his class because he knew he would see his name in the column.

After I got out of Western, I became a drifter and worked for various newspapers until I finally landed a job at the Seattle Post-Intelligencer, which no longer exists except online. Eventually I got hired at the Seattle Times. The humor columnist for its Sunday Pacific Magazine retired and they put out a contest for people to replace him. I wrote a column, sent it in (it's in this book) and it won the contest. They didn't ask for any more contestants and this column ran for the next 20 years, titled "Sunday Punch."

I didn't start my life thinking I would make my living this way. I mean, who says: "Yeah, I'm gonna be a newspaper columnist" when you talk about what you want to do when you grow up? But looking back over 40-some years, I guess it worked out that way.

I've written for money, pleasure and grades. I started out as a reporter, then became an editor and then a columnist. There are two things about being a columnist. One, I usually wrote for extra money, and two, my columns were always funny in some way.

I didn't enjoy being an editor (reporters are difficult to manage and editors didn't get to do the fun things like go outside and see the world), although editors *were* paid more.

While most of my writing has been as a reporter, where I did stories ranging from murder to government to volcanoes, I also wrote columns for extra money. Not only could I earn more that way, the columns didn't have to stick to the facts. Or anyway, they could stick to the "facts" as I saw them.

Most of my columns were called "freelance" pieces. The word "free" in the name of the work sums up the pay. It ranged from $10 a column (my first college columns) to $150 for columns published in the Seattle Homeowner's Club's monthly newsletter.

My motto was "you pay me and I'll write for you." But as you can see by the rates I charged, I didn't make a lot of money in my freelancing business. If I was fixing someone's toilet, then I would charge more for that. But charging a lot for something that I enjoyed doing and it came easy to do? What is the going rate for that? Whatever the market would bear.

I remember once an editor who wanted to hire me to write a monthly column asking how much it would cost. I said the going price was $125. You could almost hear him snort. He said that wasn't enough and raised my asking price by another 25 bucks.

The columns may have had different names, but they all had something in common. They all had something funny in them — at least they had my brand of humor, even the columns that were strictly factual, like the Just Ask Johnston columns in this book (although even there I sometimes did stretch the truth just a little bit for comic purposes).

The usual targets of my humor were either myself (that slack-jawed student Irving Bingo) or my wife, who was also known as the Truly Unpleasant Mrs. Johnston, or my children. The reason I selected these targets was because they (usually) didn't complain and there was less chance of them suing me!

– Seattle, Washington
February, 2010

In about 1973 when Steve was at the Seattle Post-Intelligencer, his editor said he would pay him $5 if he could find a suit to wear instead of his normal attire of jeans and casual clothes. This is how Steve won the challenge (and he then returned to normal dress).

The Sunday Punch Columns

PROLOGUE:
Enter the "Truly Unpleasant"

Editor's note: Since she will play such an important part in all that follows, we thought we should help set the stage by beginning our collection with an introduction to one of the stars of the show – Nancy Johnston herself. In this Sunday Punch column, Steve Johnston writes about how he met his future wife.

Love at first sight – or, how not to babble and drool over lunch

Whenever I hear someone say they don't believe in love at first sight, I have to throw back my head and laugh. Actually, I don't laugh. It's more like an Olympic elk snort, but you get the idea that I find it amusing.

With Valentine's Day raising its overly commercialized head tomorrow, I have to admit I didn't always believe in love at first sight, but that changed 15 years ago.

The other half of this story, the Truly Unpleasant Mrs. Johnston, has her own version of what happened 15 years ago, but I'm writing this and I get to tell it my way.

It started when the sheriff of Pierce County was arrested for racketeering in 1978. The sheriff and a dozen other guys went on trial and I was covering it for The Seattle Times. Because there was so much publicity about the case in Seattle, the judge decided to move it to the federal court in San Francisco.

A bunch of Seattle reporters went down to San Francisco to cover it, and we camped out in cheap little hotel rooms around the federal court. I ended up in a place across the street from the Greyhound bus depot. It was an exciting place to be, and I entertained myself trying to get to the courthouse without getting killed.

But first I must digress: There are about 60 million Catholics in this country. For some reason they all know each other or know someone who knows your mother.

You can be at a party and somebody mentions something about being a Catholic within five minutes of meeting you. I think the pope made up that rule. Pretty soon you are trading tuna-casserole stories and they're telling you about their aunt who used to weed the garden at the neighborhood parish. Before you know it, you are saying: "You're not Thelma Gulch's niece?" It turns out your uncle's best friend was married to Thelma by the priest who baptized you.

This happens all the time because, like I said, all 60 million Catholics in this country know each other or at least know someone who knows someone your mother went to school with.

I'm through digressing now, but I wanted to say this thing about Catholics because it helps explain why I believe in love at first sight.

I was stuck in the hotel across the street from the Greyhound bus depot in downtown San Francisco when an editor from The Times came into town with her husband for a rugby game.

Of course, she's Catholic and knows all the other Catholics in the United States. She called me and asked if I wanted to go to lunch with her and some friends she knew in San Francisco. It seems they all went to Seattle University together years ago because they are all Catholics and as Catholics they never lose touch with each other.

I said sure and met them at the restaurant. That's where I saw the future Mrs. Johnston for the first time. I was quite taken by her, but I didn't drool or do anything stupid right off. I was sane enough to know you can scare someone if you start babbling at them across the table.

Instead, I found out she worked for a bank and told her I needed to set up a bank account so I could cash my paycheck. I suggested we meet for lunch and open the account. Ha! It was a trick, but it worked.

Of course, by then I was already smitten, and after talking with her for a few minutes about the benefits of the American banking system, I decided I wanted to marry her.

On our first official date, I asked her to marry me. Mrs. Johnston insists that I never asked her to marry me. Instead, she says, I told her we were getting married and she better get to know me real quick because this racketeering trial was ending pretty soon and she didn't want to go to Seattle with a complete stranger. Or a complete idiot for that matter.

That was 15 years ago, and I have to admit I am still smitten by Mrs. Johnston. And that's the reason I believe in love at first sight. Tomorrow is Valentine's Day, and even though I've written that I still am smitten by Mrs. Johnston, she will expect a card and maybe some flowers.

After all, she is the Truly Unpleasant Mrs. Johnston.

— *February 13, 1994*

Nancy and Steve, 1998. She doesn't seem so unpleasant here, does she!

Chapter 1

Cruisin' Colby, and other worthless activities

Illustration Copyright © 2010 by Fred Birchman

Was that aroma a character-builder?

When I was a young adult and people asked me where I grew up, I sometimes lied and said I was from Seattle. Actually, I was from Everett. But Seattle sounded more sophisticated than Everett. Saying you were from Seattle made it sound like you were from an exotic foreign country compared with saying you were from Everett.

That was especially true many years ago, when the pulp mills were running full blast and — right after you said you were from Everett — people would say: "Boy, what's that smell?!"

Certain parts of Everett smelled like rotten eggs. If you were driving through and happened to catch a bad wind blowing your way on the north side of town, the inside of your car would smell like you had eaten some bad bean dip.

There were three ways to handle the awkwardness of the smell. You could explain to a visitor that the odor came from the pulp mills making paper. Or you could say it was the smell of money, because you worked in the mills during the summer and mill work paid pretty good. Or you could say you were from Seattle.

Today the pulp mills are gone and so is the stink. Now when you admit you're from Everett you don't have to make excuses for the way your hometown smells.

But people will still say something negative about the place. Certain towns get a bad reputation, and the folks who live in them can't shake it.

If you say you are from Renton or Tacoma, two working-class towns where the cars and trucks have big tires, women have big hair and guys have big attitudes, then someone is going to crack wise about your hometown. In the old days, a wisecrack about the old hometown got you a clip in the chops. But us guys from those towns are more worldly nowadays, and don't go around smacking people upside their heads. Even if they deserve it.

In the past few years, the hometown boys from Everett have been doing the town proud. Just look at the three head coaches for the major football teams in Washington: They all graduated from Everett High School. At one time we all probably cruised Colby Avenue together.

Matter of fact, Dennis Erickson (Seahawks coach) and Mike Price (Washington State University coach) graduated at the same time I did from Everett High while Jim Lambright (University of Washington coach) got out of there a few years before us.

Some people may notice a trend here. They might even think that growing up with the smell of the pulp mills filtering through your nose makes you want to put on a helmet and go smashing into people.

I'll admit that the smell of rotten eggs didn't do much for your disposition. But other people from Everett did more than learn how to toss around an inflated pig bladder. (In Everett, we used the real thing for a football.)

Another guy from my high-school class, Chad Henry, went on to write the longest-running play ever in Seattle, "Angry Housewives." It lingered around town longer than the smell from some of those pulp mills.

Today this magazine has a story about an Everett High boy named Chuck Close who went away to New York and became a famous artist.

But he's coming back to town for a museum show and if you could get close enough, you might still smell the pulp mills.

Like they say: You can take the boy out of Everett, but you can't take Everett out of the boy.

– December 6, 1998

Pour it on – or, it's plain the rain is mainly for the brave

I'm one of those unusual people. I like it when it rains. When it doesn't rain for a long time, like two weeks or so, I start missing it and I begin getting nervous. That run of dry days in July got me worrying.

Then I read a story with good news. It said the weather folks were predicting the next 100 years were going to be exceptionally wet. I had to share the good news with the Truly Unpleasant Mrs. Johnston. "Dear," I called out to the kitchen where Mrs. Johnston was busy avoiding me, "it says here that we are going to get more rain than usual. And not just next year. It says it's for the next 100 years! That gives me something to look forward to."

I couldn't quite make out what Mrs. Johnston replied because she was banging the pots and pans so loudly, but I believe she was not sharing my excitement at the prospect of a century of rain.

The problem with your attitude toward rain is that it depends on where you were raised. Mrs. Johnston was raised near San Francisco, where they don't get much rain. They have their weather issues, like fog, but they don't have much rain. So when it rains for two weeks straight, Mrs. Johnston tends to get a little testy.

But I grew up under Northwest skies. For an idea how deep my rain roots run, until I was 7 years old I lived on the edge of Olympic National Park. One of the draws to the park is the Olympic Rain Forest. To get the title of "rain forest," a place has to get at least 6 feet of rain a year. That's a measly 72 inches. In the Olympic Rain Forest, the average rainfall is 144 inches a year. That's 12 feet of water falling on you in as many months.

When it really pours in the Olympic Rain Forest, you are talking about 14 to 16 feet of rain. If it rained every day of the year in the rain forest, it would be a half-inch or so every day. But it didn't rain every day in my birth place. It came as a mist and moved on to drizzle, broken up by cloud bursts so heavy it was like being hit with a fire hose, followed by a steady downpour and wrapping up the rest of the week with a forecast of cloudy days mixed with showers.

When my family moved to Everett, it was a shock to my system. Not only did I move from having no neighbors to living in an actual city, I also went to a place where it didn't rain all that much, maybe just five months out of the year. It hardly got your hair wet.

If you grow up in the Rain Culture, then you become a Rain Warrior. If you move here, then you get to be a Rain Weenie. A Rain Warrior doesn't own an umbrella. If someone gives the Warrior an umbrella, it is kept near the front door to be lent to the Rain Weenie when it starts to drizzle.

A Rain Warrior will wear a hat (maybe a ball cap with a local team name on it) and a jacket that is waterproof and has a hood on it. But nothing else to signal the Warrior needs any sort of shield to face the deluge. If you look in a Rain Warrior's front-room closet, you will find different coats with hoods, different colors, different weights, different styles. But all good to wear in the rain.

A Rain Weenie will go outside in the rain — but *only* if dressed to face a Nor'wester (that's another rain storm). The Weenie will carry an umbrella. It may not be used but it will be carried, just in case.

There is hope for the Rain Weenie. I've been married to one for almost 30 years — and last month she left her umbrella in the hall closet. Maybe this month she will leave her rubber boots next to her umbrella.

– October 21, 2007

Thrill of waxing wanes over the years

When I was about 10 years old and growing up in Everett, I discovered that the height of hilarity was soaping someone's windows if they didn't have the good sense to be home on Halloween.

And if this person had made the further mistake of not being home for two years running, the windows wouldn't be soaped. No, I would use a candle and wax them. Wax was harder to get off a window, but some of my meaner friends would run the blunt end of a candle across the screen door.

The next day we could walk down the street and see which family wasn't home on Halloween night. There would be big soapy and waxy Xs across their windows and maybe the screen door. You could get the soap off the window with a little water; the wax came off with a razor blade, but a waxed screen door took months to scrub off because you had to get the candle wax out of all those little holes.

Like I said, I thought this was real funny when I was 10 years old. A few decades later, I don't think I would find it quite as amusing. Instead of the old grouch down the block, it would be me who would be spending next Sunday morning scrubbing candle wax or soap swipes off the windows.

I'm sure the little monsters from hell who did it would think it was the height of hilarity to wax my windows, but I don't think I would shake my head in a kindly Old Grouch Down The Block fashion and mutter, "Those kids! I remember doing that when I was a kid." No, it would be more like: "Call the cops! I want those little vandals doing some hard time!"

The reason I bring this up is because a week from today some gentle reader may go to his/her front door and find a giant X on the front window or even worse, some nasty four-letter word in candle wax that will be there until Christmas and the neighborhood carolers will stop in the middle of "Silent Night" and hurry away talking about those "obscene people in that house."

This person will, of course, blame me for this act of vandalism, saying that if I hadn't written about how much fun it was to grow up in Everett and write giant Xs on people's windows, then nobody would have thought about doing it. If I hadn't planted the idea in this social misfit's tiny brain, he would have gone on to other ways to entertain himself — like leaning a garbage can against the front door, knocking and then running far enough away so he could see the surprised reaction on your face when you open the door and garbage comes spilling across your living room.

No, the reason I brought this subject up wasn't because my windows have ever been waxed or soaped. Garbage cans have never been placed against my front door nor have paper bags full of dog poop ever been

11

lit on fire and put on the front porch so I'll come out and stamp on the burning bag, only to find dog poop squished all over the place. Nor have I driven down the street to see a neighbor's tree covered with enough toilet paper so it looks like a float in the Seafair parade.

(There is a famous story told by grandfathers all over the country about Halloween and outhouses where the kids go to a farmer's outhouse and push it over the hill. As it rolls down the hill, the kids realize that Old Farmer Brown was sitting in the outhouse. Everett, thank goodness, had indoor plumbing.)

But I did get to thinking about those juvenile pranks my friends and I used to pull in the name of fun when I came out to my car and found that some juvenile delinquent who should be breaking rocks on a chain gang had gotten a can of that stuff called Silly String (it shoots out a skinny string like shaving foam) and walked down the street squirting the stuff on the side of cars. There was a wiggly stream of Silly String for about a block of cars.

It was a hot day and the string had dried on hard. Most of it came off with hand brushing, but some had to be scrubbed off. As I scrubbed it off, I thought about all those screen doors and windows in Everett that I had waxed on Halloween and thought it was pretty funny.

If any of those people are still waiting behind their front doors with a baseball bat and hoping I'll return, I must say I'm sorry and promise never to do it again.

I won't, however, come to your house next Sunday and wash off the big Xs.

— October 25, 1992

Eric and Dad hanging out, circa 1978

A school for fathers? I could use it.

When I was a little kid, I thought my father could fix anything. If a wheel came off my wagon, I knew he could fix it. If the chain fell off the bicycle, he would take out his Craftsman tools and put it back on.

I would watch him and wonder how he knew what to do. Was there a secret Father's School they send these guys before they become fathers?

When I got a little older, I always figured he could fix anything but it was still a mystery how he knew how to do it. By then I was convinced there was that secret school he attended because I had a hard time stumping him with some problem.

I remember one time coming into the family home in Everett and telling my father that my '46 Chevy wouldn't start. He never even put down the evening paper when he answered.

"What's it do when you turn the key?" he asked. I said it made a clicking and "clunking" sound.

"Sounds like your solenoid," he grunted. "Probably stuck. Open your hood and it's on the left side. On top of the starter. Tap it a couple of times with a screwdriver."

I don't think he even stopped reading the paper while passing along this piece of advice. I didn't know what a solenoid was, but I went outside and opened the hood of the Chevy. I found the starter (my father once told me you could always find the starter at the end of a battery cable, another piece of fatherly information casually passed along that would last a lifetime) and there was a little cylinder-shaped thing on top of the starter. I gave it a good whack with my screwdriver and got back into the Chevy. It started right up.

I wondered how he was able to do that. I mean, did he memorize an auto-repair book, just waiting for someone to ask what it meant when you turned a key in a '46 Chevy and the only sound you heard was "clunk"?

But he was a father and fathers are expected to know stuff like that. It would be years before I realized that they learned just by being alive and not looking away when someone showed them how to do something.

There are drawbacks to growing up in a house with a father who can explain how to fix a car or put the chain on a bicycle without putting down the newspaper. It sets a high standard to follow.

For one thing, I never saw a repairman come into our house to fix anything. There were no plumbers or carpenters wandering around our house with a bag of tools, looking concerned about some repair job.

When something broke down in the house, it was understood that my father would fix it. After all, that's what fathers do because they went to that secret Father's School on weekends. I remember one of the rules my father used to tell me: "You just have to be a little smarter than the thing you are working on."

(His other rules include: "Measure twice and cut once," "Always buy the worst house in the best neighborhood" and "You'll never get rich working for wages." These are rules I think they teach at the Father's School and if you follow them, you won't go wrong.)

Nowadays, things are more complicated than when I was growing up. I don't think cars even have solenoids anymore and if they do, I can't find them when I open the hood. The Truly Unpleasant Mrs. Johnston drives a van that has its engine turned sideways, for crying out loud! Plus there is some kind of computer stuff in there that should have a warning on it that says: "Touch me and it will cost $600 to fix."

My father died 11 years ago, so I don't know if he would say his being-smarter-than-what-you're-working-on rule would still apply. There are some appliances in our house that I believe are smarter than me.

Even stuff that doesn't plug into the wall is dangerous to fix (because of my early training, I try to fix anything that breaks). One of the kids' videotapes broke the other day and she brought it to me to fix. I figured I was smarter than the tape, so I took out several tiny screws and removed the cover.

My '46 Chevy went "clunk" when it didn't work and I fixed it with a screwdriver. The VCR tape went "ping" when I took it apart with a screwdriver and now it *really* doesn't work.

For this Father's Day, I'm hoping my kids will pay the tuition at Father's School.

– June 19, 1994

What goes around comes around. Don't believe it? Just ask my mom.

When we had a couple inches of snow at the end of January, the Johnston children took their sleds out to the hill, got into a snowball fight and let one sled go down the hill so it smacked a neighbor's car.

No damage done, but I was telling my mother about her misbehaving grandchildren who would do something so irresponsible as throw snowballs at each other while on a sled and then let the sled go while they returned fire.

"That's nothing compared to what you used to do," my mother said, launching into one of my childhood adventures with my brothers while growing up on Colby Avenue in beautiful Everett.

The trouble with mothers is that they never forget a thing. I can't remember if my mother ever actually made that parent curse of "I hope you have children just like you" but I know she must have thought of it a few times over the years.

It's payback time for parents when they get a phone call from one of their children, complaining about something one of their offspring did and hoping for a little sympathy. But instead of hearing "I don't know how you are to put up with those children. You must be a saint," you hear your mother snorting with laughter.

"Do you remember that time you put the billfold on the sidewalk and hooked it to a fish line?" my mother was saying after I told her about the sled incident. "When someone came along to pick it up, you pulled in the wallet and had them chase you?"

Or how about the time I threw the hub cap behind a passing car and when the driver got out to pick up the hub cap he thought came off his car, a brother or two and I would run out, grab the hub cap and go running through the back yards and across the garage rooftops of Colby Avenue?

With any luck the driver would give chase and try to get back what he thought was his hub cap, but he couldn't move faster than a bunch of boys who knew the neighborhood alleys and rooftops like they knew their own back yard.

Or the time one Johnston brother got on the shoulders of another Johnston brother, put on a long black coat and a horrible Halloween mask, and went lumbering across Colby Avenue like some kind of demented giant, forcing cars to stop and then peering into the drivers' windows?

Actually, I didn't do the giant routine. That was something done by my younger brothers, but I always found it extremely amusing to hear them tell about the reaction of the drivers.

Or the time the Johnston brothers decided to build an outdoor swimming pool, so they dug a huge hole in the back yard and filled it up with the garden hose and were surprised to see the swimming pool didn't actually work as planned? Instead of a swimming pool, we ended up with a mud pit that we wallowed in like pigs.

My mother also likes to tell me about my Everett High School counselor who reads this column and tells my mother she is surprised I didn't end up in prison.

You can see there isn't much sympathy coming from my mother when I mention some of the antics of her grandchildren. Whatever they do, there seems to be a story about my brothers and me that will top it.

I mentioned this to the Truly Unpleasant Mrs. Johnston the other day and said I was glad my mother didn't find out about the time the Johnston brothers stood in the back yard and one of us fired an arrow into the air. The idea was to stand very still and hope the arrow didn't come through your skull. Anyone who ran for cover under the carport lost the contest.

The Truly Unpleasant Mrs. Johnston agreed it was best that my mother didn't know that was going on, and she thought it was a miracle my mother survived her children's childhood.

– March 24, 1996

Johnston children living up to Grandma's prediction, 1990

Chapter 2
Krazy Kids and Fatherhood

Illustration Copyright © 2010 by Fred Birchman

A new class of outcasts: Meet the SILKs!

Editor's note: This is a very special column – the first Sunday Punch column Steve wrote for Pacific magazine (now Pacific Northwest) at The Seattle Times.

I have four kids.

There was a time when that statement wouldn't have raised an eyebrow. But these days people look at me like I have no control over my bodily functions. Well, OK, I didn't have any control until recently.

Now that things are under control, I still find myself an outcast in society. I can only look down my nose at my dentist who has eight kids and has lost complete control of his bodily functions.

There is a name for people like me. Most people have heard of **DINKs** *(Double Income, No Kids)*. I am a **SILK.** That stands for *Single Income, Lots of Kids.*

Here is the difference between the two groups:

DINKs go to dinner at restaurants with candle light and soft music playing in the background. They laugh and whisper over a bottle of French wine.

SILKs have dinner at Pizza and Pipes and listen to music provided by a man playing an organ the size of a small aircraft carrier. **SILKs**

hope they don't set the table on fire. They yell and scream over a pitcher of Coke and use what's left of the Coke to put out the fire.

DINKs go on vacation to some remote Mexican coast villa where they water-ski behind a boat and then float up in the air attached to a parachute. They wave at their happy mates sitting on the shore under a large umbrella. Their drinks have matching umbrellas.

SILKs go on vacation to some remote campground on the Olympic Peninsula with the kids jammed in the back of the nine-passenger Country Squire. The only thing floating out the back is a helium balloon purchased at Pizza and Pipes the night before. Mom and Dad are waving but they are waving rolled-up newspapers at the kids who are fighting in the backseat.

DINKs like to shop at downtown stores where the sales clerks talk like they have clothespins attached to their noses and soft music plays in the background. The dresses don't go above size 6, and the men's pants only come in waist size of 32 and smaller. The shoes are leather, and the clothing is all natural fabric. The labels are in a foreign language. Some of the pants are baggy, but only on purpose.

SILKs like to shop at Chubby and Tubby's where they can trade in the kids' old tennis shoes for a $5 discount on another pair. They usually go to shops where the clerks won't talk to them, if a clerk can be found at all. If there is any noise in the background, it is a loudspeaker announcing the latest special under the flashing blue lights. The shoes are either rubber or plastic, and the clothes are all man-made products, and the labels are from Korea. The pants are also baggy, but they can be taken in.

DINKs have hobbies. They like to refurbish old apartment buildings into condos. They like to take art classes at night school and contact 25,000-year-old spirits after class. They build ships inside bottles and take up playing the classical guitar. They like to collect coins and things called commodities.

SILKs have hobbies. They like to spend Friday night trying to put together the toy that came in the McDonald's kids' Meal Deal. They also like to turn a clean house into a wreck. They try to contact a 67-year-old grandmother who has a recording that says, "I raised mine. You raise yours." They try to take the car keys out of the toilet. They like to collect coins from under couch cushions after visitors leave.

DINKs like to have quiet evenings at home. They like to sit in front of the fireplace and sip a glass of white wine with classical music playing softly in the background and the city lights twinkling below their balcony. They like to talk about politics and good literature.

SILKs have no choice but to have noisy evenings at home. They try to keep the kids out of the fireplace, and, if it is available, they will drink a bottle of wine. They don't use glasses. They listen to Tim Noah sing about furry monsters while watching the twinkle from the Death Ray guns from the Masters of the Universe collection. They like to talk about day care and Dr. Seuss.

Finally, **DINKs** say things like "You can never be too rich or too thin. And you can never have enough of everything."

SILKs say: "You can never be too rested or have enough help. And you can never have enough duct tape."

– September 11, 1988

'Are we there yet?' On family road trips, whining is a tradition

By the time you read this, the Johnston family will be on its annual "fun" vacation. And if you are reading this around 11 a.m. on Sunday, I should be fairly hysterical.

Maybe you can hear me scream. We should be somewhere in southern Oregon and I'll be yelling something like: "You kids stop wrestling back there RIGHT NOW or I'll pull over and do some real wrestling with you!" I like to alternate this statement with the following: "The next rest stop isn't for another 200 miles, SO JUST HOLD IT!"

This is how the annual Johnston "fun" vacation goes. By the way, it always goes the same way. It's a family tradition.

The Truly Unpleasant Mrs. Johnston gets to select a destination. For some reason, she always selects the San Francisco area. She claims she picks this part of the country because her family lives there and, for some unexplained reason, she likes to see them.

With the difficult part out of the way, the next decision is how to get there. This is also fairly easy. We've done this many times. We always

23

drive. It's 905 miles and it takes 15 hours to drive, including three pit stops.

Every year we like to pretend we can afford to fly down. We sit at the kitchen table and count the number of children we have to take to California, and two adults. Then we check the Sunday travel section to see how much it would cost to fly an adult and a child to San Francisco.

After we write the ticket price down on a paper napkin, we multiply and come up with a number. I always get to say the same thing. "It's too expensive. Looks like we'll have to drive down this year," I say.

Like this is a big surprise. But it's the only input I have in deciding the annual vacation. That and driving the van.

The only change to these plans is when Mrs. Johnston and I debate whether to make the 900-mile journey in one day or take a more leisurely drive down the Highway to Hell by stopping at some over-priced motel along the way.

In keeping with the family tradition, I say it would be easier to drive straight through.

We can leave at 2 in the morning and the kids will sleep through Washington, waking up as we pass under the sign that says "Welcome To Oregon" at the Columbia River. We can hear the first "Are we there yet?" It will be the first of 3 million "Are we there yet?" questions.

The I-Got-To-Go-To-The-Bathroom routine doesn't start until we're through Portland and pass the sign that says "243 miles to next rest area." There is a brief struggle over blankets and pillows in the back, and one kid punches another kid for invading his space.

We fuel up in Salem and make a pit stop at McDonald's. Mrs. Johnston likes to ask if I want her to take over driving. She always knows I will give the same answer that I give when we are lost and she asks if we should pull over and ask some complete stranger for directions.

"No, thanks," I always say. "I'm doing fine." It's a traditional answer.

With the right planning, we don't stop again until we go through the fruit inspectors at the California border where those lovable children like to say we are smuggling fruit. Ha! If these kids had their way, fruit would be banned from the country.

With the proper timing, we can get to San Francisco in time for the afternoon rush hour and be stuck on one of the bridges for a couple of hours.

When we finally arrive at my mother-in-law's house, my legs are like rubber and I collapse in the driveway.

In two weeks, my legs are working well enough to work the pedals on the van and we hit the road again. We reverse the journey.

After all, it's a family tradition.

– July 23, 1995

Kitchen caper

The other day I heard a noise in the kitchen. It wasn't a loud noise, like someone shouting or hitting something. It was . . . well, a chomping noise, sort of like when your dog gets a shoe and starts chewing on it real quietly so you won't hear it.

When I went to investigate I found a gaggle of teenagers standing around the kitchen counter. The gaggle was made up of teenage boys and I recognized most of them as friends of the Johnston teenage boys.

What was interesting about this group was that they weren't saying much. It's always unnerving when teenagers don't talk. I don't mean talk to an adult. My kids haven't said much to me since they hit their teen years. But I've found they like to talk to each other.

Of course when they do, it is mainly conversation that sounds like this: "Like you know what I mean, like you know?" But these teens weren't even carrying on a deep conversation about the various ways they could use the phrase "like you know" in a single sentence.

These teens were just crowded around the kitchen counter. They seemed to be looking at something but I couldn't see what it was because these kids were the size of linebackers and they were blocking my view.

(I must digress here and ask a question. Have you noticed how big kids are nowadays? I mean, the average teenager towers over his or her parents. The Truly Unpleasant Mrs. Johnston is the shortest person in our family. Even our daughter was taller than Mrs. Johnston by the time she hit 13. Either we are feeding these kids too well or parents are shrinking, thanks to a science experiment the kids are doing in biology when they are supposed to be studying sex education. This is just a thought and now I'm finished digressing.)

Finally, I got a quick look at the countertop to see what was holding the gaggle's attention. I knew it couldn't be something like a textbook or an interesting article from the newspaper. No, what had grabbed these guys' attention was a cake I had baked, coated with fudge frosting and put on the kitchen counter to cool. I figured I would have some later that night.

I figured wrong.

The cake was in an 11-by-17-inch pan and was probably still warm and fragrant. As you know, it takes only one teen to smell food; soon the whole gaggle will be moving purposefully in one direction.

It didn't surprise me that when I looked into the cake pan, most of the cake was gone. What surprised me was the way it had been eaten.

You know how some kids will eat a sandwich without eating the crust? That was what the cake looked like.

All the center was gone, but a border of about one inch ran around the edge of the pan. Apparently the gaggle cut pieces out of the center and worked over to the edge until they became frightened at the thought of eating the cake's crust.

If the kids felt guilty about eating the family dessert, they didn't say so. One of them mumbled, "Good, like, cake, you know," as they walked out.

But here is where age has it over youth when it comes to cakes. When you put frosting on a cake, the frosting is always harder to spread in the center so the center always gets less frosting than the edges.

The gaggle may have eaten most of the cake, but in their excitement and inexperience, they overlooked the best, most thickly frosted part.

At least that's what I told myself as I ate the cake's crust.

— January 30, 2000

Wait a minute. How did they get so young?

The other day, Mrs. Johnston and I went to a wedding. When I saw the young couple standing together in front of the minister, I told Mrs. Johnston that they didn't look old enough to get a driver's license, much less a marriage license. "Be quiet," the Truly Unpleasant Mrs. Johnston hissed.

The youth of the newlyweds wasn't the only thing that got my attention. When we went into the church basement for the reception, I noticed something else. There were no old people in the crowd.

I remember weddings and family gatherings over the years, and the one thing I could always count on was seeing old people at them. These were lumpy guys in baggy suits and gray-haired women in flowery dresses. They seemed to know everyone in the crowd, and you could always count on them to smack you on the back and leave sweet-smelling powder on your shoulder after pinching your cheeks and screaming that you looked like some long-dead relative.

At the Johnston-family gatherings, you could always count on Uncle Art and Aunt Alice. I knew they weren't my aunt and uncle because they weren't sister or brother to my mother or father. But they showed up every time the family got together, pinched our cheeks, ate the food and told stories about dead relatives.

At this particular wedding, I looked over the crowd to see this family's version of Uncle Art and Aunt Alice, but I didn't see any old couples wandering through the crowd, pinching cheeks and telling stories. When I pointed this out to Mrs. Johnston, she looked at me like I had lost my mind.

"*We* are the old people, dear," the Truly Unpleasant Mrs. Johnston said.

Wow! I had never thought of myself as an Uncle Art, but I suppose to a 20-something I look like an old man in a bad-fitting suit. I stopped myself from calling any of the youngsters taking to the dance floor "those young whippersnappers," but I felt like it.

Life is funny that way. Has this ever happened to you? You go to bed feeling like a teenager and you wake up with a wife, four kids and a mortgage the size of some Third World country. It happened to me while I wasn't paying attention.

To top it off, by the time you read this column I will take on a new title. A young woman will identify me as her father-in-law. It seems one of the three Johnston boys has convinced a young lady that marrying into the Johnston clan is a good idea. Fortunately, I have managed to keep this young woman from having any heart-to-heart talks with Mrs. Johnston. But I have caught Mrs. Johnston "mouthing" a word of advice to the bride-to-be.

"Run," Mrs. Johnston seems to be saying. "Run."

But I think the young lady thought her future mother-in-law was only joking. When Mrs. Johnston left the table to do something in the kitchen, I made a little joke about the warning.

"You know your future mother-in-law is nuts," I said light-heartedly. She nodded in agreement but looked worried.

This young woman seems to be fairly stable, though, and maybe she can take it.

The wedding is going to be in her home town of 900, in Montana. She hired a local guy to cater the wedding feast, and naturally he wanted to know how many people were coming to the reception. About 180, she replied.

That will be 24 feet of food, the guy said. Not 180 dinners. Not 100 steak and 80 chicken dinners. Just 24 feet of food. (I'm hoping the 24 feet will be divided into sections like vegetables, salads and main dishes, but I cannot say for sure.)

The only thing I know for sure is that I plan to eat a foot of food and make people think Mrs. Johnston and I are Uncle Art and Aunt Alice. It's a family tradition.

– October 3, 2004

Tricked again by man's best friend

Just the other day I realized my dog was smarter than me.

This doesn't come as any surprise to the Truly Unpleasant Mrs. Johnston, who also says the family cat is smarter than me. But it's taken me a few years to come to this conclusion. For the first eight years of his life, I thought Rex was addled. He didn't show much enthusiasm for things most dogs like to do, such as play "fetch," that mindless game where you throw a ball or stick and the dog chases it and brings it back. Rex would play, but only if the item being thrown had meat attached to it.

There is one trick that Rex is good at doing. When I say "Sit" or "Lie down," he can do that because he's already sitting or lying down. He also knows the question: "You want a treat?" But if it requires doing something for the treat, he usually passes on the treat. Instead, he waits patiently until you get tired of holding the treat and throw it to him.

So rather than being trained to do tricks, Rex has trained us to do tricks. His favorite is: "Fetch me a treat."

Rex is a Labrador. I like Labs for many reasons, but one of the big ones is that they are good with kids. Over the years, I've seen my kids climb over, under and across our Labradors. When the children were little, they would grab ahold of the dog's droopy ears and swing on them. The poor dog would just have a look on his face of, "When is this ever going to end?"

I got hooked on Labs when I was growing up in Everett and we had a golden Lab named Butch. Unlike Rex, Butch was a functioning dog who could do all the things regular dogs do: run, fetch, sit, stand and so on. We never expected our dogs to do anything useful like hunt or get dead ducks out of the water, mainly because we didn't hunt. I always hoped that our Labs would get help if any of us ever fell down a well or got trapped under a fallen tree like in the TV show "Lassie." ("Go get Pa, Butch," we'd croak out.) But no one ever fell down a well or got trapped under a tree.

I can only remember two negative experiences with Butch. Like most Labradors, Butch liked to swim. Once when we were swimming with him, Butch decided he was too tired to continue paddling. He needed a place to climb on to rest. Unfortunately, the nearest object was my brother, Bill, and Butch climbed up his back. Not only did he dig his claws into Bill's back but we were swimming in saltwater and you could hear the screaming for miles.

The other negative experience was our own fault. We used to play a game with Butch where we threw something to him and he would keep it away from us. It was usually a stick or ball. But one time he got ahold of my fancy-pants Little League glove and started running around the yard with it in his mouth. Of course we started chasing him. And, of course, Butch started running with my glove. He was playing his favorite game. He would run to a corner of the yard, sit down and start shaking and chewing on the glove. We'd come after him, screaming and yelling. Butch would throw the glove in the air, catch it and race off to another part of the yard, a pack of kids hot on his tail.

When I finally got my glove back, it was chewed up pretty good. But Butch had enjoyed himself.

When we got Rex, he was stepping in for another black Lab, Duke, who had died of old age. Maybe it was because Duke was so old at the end that we forgot dogs are supposed to do more than sleep and eat.

Rex was a perfect replacement for the old dog. He settled into Duke's spot and took a nap.

– November 12, 2006

On the road again (is something gross)

While on a long drive, my wife, the Ever-Observant Mrs. Johnston, likes to point out interesting road kill she spots on the highway.

The children, who have been busy in the back seat poking each other and trying to make the youngest one cry, will stop their merrymaking when they hear their mother say something like this:

"Oh, look at that poor dead squirrel."

Whatever it was on the highway isn't anymore. At 60 miles an hour, it's difficult to tell what anything is anyway. All I saw was something that looked like a furry Frisbee with four legs and a tail sticking out. It could have even been a piece of rubber that blew off an 18-wheeler.

But the words "Oh, look at that poor dead ..." is enough to get the kids to stop fighting, poking each other in the ribs and shouting, "Mom, Tim is sticking out his tongue at me." This statement makes their heads spin around like those little dogs you see in the back seats of cars.

The following conversation takes place:

"What?!" the kids scream.

"Oh, I thought I saw some little animal alongside the road," says the saddened Mrs. Johnston.

"Where?" the kids scream. Now their heads are screwing around like Linda Blair in "The Exorcist."

"Oh, back there. You can't see it anymore," says the Truly Unpleasant Mrs. Johnston. "It was just some unfortunate creature who wandered in the road."

"We want to see!" the kids scream. "We didn't see it!"

Now they are really worked up. Next to a good car wreck, there is nothing more exciting to break up a long car ride than interesting road kill.

"Dad! Turn around and go back!" the little rubberneckers in the back seat start screaming. "Turn around! We want to see!"

I must digress here to ask: What planet do children come from anyway? As far as I know, I have never heard of a parent who would drive to the nearest exit, cross over the freeway to the exit heading in the opposite direction and drive back to some exit 10 miles down the road so their kids can see some flattened squirrel on the side of the road.

If there is such a parent, then that parent should be arrested.

But it is always worth the chance, the kids figure, that their parents were replaced overnight by parents from the evil planet Zen-Zar where they actually enjoy looking at interesting road kill. Matter of fact, these parents plan vacation tours around the subject.

Not these parents on this planet and not this trip. When told that we are continuing on, two of the kids start arguing the point like $25-an-hour lawyers and the littlest one starts crying like her heart will break.

A summary of their arguments goes something like this: "I didn't get to see it! The boys always get to see everything!" "You never do anything for me. You are always doing something for Molly because she's the youngest." "You bought new tennis shoes for the other kids, and you didn't get anything for me."

Several miles down the road things get back to normal. The kids are in the back seat, punching each other on the arm, making faces at cars passing us and shouting, "When are we going to get there?"

I return to being hypnotized by the road and the Ever-Observant Mrs. Johnston resumes her post to watch out for anything interesting on the side of the road. All is right with the world.

Until I hear Mrs. Johnston say something under her breath. Normally, we have to shout to be heard over the noise in the mini-van, and when we shout for the kids to stop fighting, they say they can't hear us.

But a parent saying something in a whisper brings everything to a halt. Poking stops and a cry stops in the middle of working its way up the ladder to a good scream. All that can be heard is the tires rolling on the black top.

A voice comes from the back seat. "What did you say?" it asks.

"Oh, nothing much," says the Ever-Observant Mrs. Johnston. "I just thought I saw Elvis go by us in that station wagon."

Even before one of the kids can say "Where?!" I floor it, and the chase is on.

– November 15, 1992

The gift that got away: a cautionary tale

It's getting to be that time of year when you start thinking about getting something special for the kids this Christmas.

Here are two words you might want to consider to use as a guide for your holiday gift buying. The first word is: hamster. The second word is: don't. If you need any help putting these two words together in selecting your Christmas gift, this may help: DON'T BUY A HAMSTER!!

Actually, buying a hamster isn't that expensive. You can pick one up for five or six bucks. If you want to keep the hamster in your bathrobe pocket and try to feed it table scraps like the family dog, then you will be out only the six bucks.

Of course the hamster will escape from your bathrobe pocket and you'll get blamed by the kids for losing it. So you will have to buy another hamster. That's another $6.

Only this time, you will have to lay out $30 or $40 for a hamster cage. After you buy the hamster cage, one of your friends will say something like this: "Oh, you have a hamster? We have a cage you could have for ... ummmm ... 20 bucks. We used to have a hamster but the kids lost ... ummmm ... interest in it."

But it's too late to get a free cage because you just bought one and anyway you wonder why the kids would ever lose ... ummmm ... interest in a hamster. After bringing the new cage home, you find it takes up most of the top of the dresser. It will also have a small house inside so the hamster will have somewhere to stay during the day. A hamster, by the way, is a nocturnal animal, which means that unlike most creatures in your house, this animal is like a teenager and it's up all night.

Fortunately, inside the $40 cage is a wheel where the hamster can climb inside and start running. It will run and run and run. It will run all night. At the first light, the hamster will stop running and go to sleep. But as you lay in the darkness, listening to the hamster run and run and run in its little wheel, you wonder why scientists haven't figured out a way to hook up a series of hamsters running in spinning wheels to those generators in the Bonneville Power Administration and just shut down the power dams on the Columbia River.

Meanwhile, the hamster's owner has been down to your bedroom several dozen times during the night to announce that the hamster is keeping this small person awake and you had better do something about it real soon.

It doesn't matter because on the second night of hamster ownership, the hamster escapes from its cage and is now somewhere in the house, setting up a birthing room with the other hamster that escaped from your bathrobe pocket.

Of course it's your fault the hamster escaped and you have to buy another hamster. After all, there is that $40 hamster cage taking up most of the dresser top and it would be a shame to waste all the money.

After laying out another $6 for a new hamster at the hamster store, you put it in a carrying case about the size of a shoe box. This is when you discover something else really remarkable about hamsters. They are kind of like those guys in the movie "The Great Escape." They can chew and tunnel through anything.

As you pull in front of your house, all the kids are on the sidewalk, jumping up and down in excitement because you are bringing home another hamster. Only when you pick up the shoe box with the new hamster you notice it's pretty light and you happen to remember you didn't hear it rustling around inside the box for the last couple of miles anyway (you thought it was asleep. Ha!) and now you see a hole the size of your thumb in one corner of the box.

Of course the hamster has escaped. Now you have two in the house and one in your car. None in the $40 hamster cage eating the $10 worth of hamster food you bought or rolling around the $15 plastic see-through ball or driving the little electric $17 hamster car that the kids insisted that all hamsters had to have. This hamster idea is starting to look like a $100 pain.

Here is your choice: You can buy another hamster or wait until a friend buys one and then say your kids ... ummmm ... lost interest in their hamster and you have this cage and electric car.

– *December 6, 1992*

One of Molly's favorite spots to listen to a story, 1987

The family that vacations together learns why you don't do it often

Some time back, I met a guy who had 10 brothers and sisters. They lived in a small house near Kirkland where several brothers slept in one bedroom and the sisters slept in another. The guy moved out when he hit 18 and I asked him how he liked living by himself.

"I didn't know it could be so quiet," he said.

That statement came back to me when I went on a vacation with my family. Not with just the Truly Unpleasant Mrs. Johnston and our kids, but all of the Johnstons. At least the Johnstons belonging to that human unit people call "the immediate family," which includes three brothers, a sister, their spouses and various kids.

Altogether, there are 28 of us.

The group vacation was my mother's idea. Maybe she got tired of cooking dinner for this bunch on Sundays and figured a family vacation to Disney World in Florida would get her out of the kitchen for a while.

She said it would be her treat and who could pass up a deal like that? My mother said she would rather spend her money now than leave it for her kids to blow on something crazy like vacations to Florida in the middle of the winter.

The nice part of this vacation – besides the part where my mother picked up the tab – was that I didn't have to do anything. It was a vacation produced by Walt Disney, with my younger sister doing the grunt work of getting all the tickets and worrying whether her brothers would be in the right place at the right time to catch a plane or boat.

Looking back on it, it's amazing that this huge group of people was able to meet at Sea-Tac Airport in the middle of the night, fly clear across the country and spend eight days first in a crowded theme park, then on a ship with visits to foreign countries thrown in, without getting into a fight, getting lost or losing a kid.

When we were younger, my brothers and I were not able to travel from Everett to Seattle to visit my grandmother without punching and pinching each other while sitting in the rear seat of the family station wagon. Now our kids punch and pinch each other while we tell them to settle down.

The other amazing thing is that while Disney World is a huge place with a half-dozen theme parks spread out over most of middle Florida, you couldn't go anywhere without running into another Johnston. It was like that theory says: If you sit in one spot long enough, eventually everyone you know in the world will walk by.

One night, Mrs. Johnston and I were having dinner at one of the many Disney-theme restaurants. We looked up and saw my mother at the next table. Within a few minutes, a brother and his wife came wandering in and then some of their kids turned up. Before we could order dessert, there were Johnstons throughout the place. It was like throwing bread crumbs off the back porch and watching birds come flocking in.

In fact, it was like having Sunday dinner at my mother's place in Everett.

The same thing happened when we got on the Disney ship. There may have been a couple thousand people on the ship, but if you sat down somewhere, you wouldn't be alone for very long. Some relative would wander by every few minutes.

The only Johnstons we didn't run into on land or sea were our own children. It wasn't that we didn't cross paths all the time. But every time I spotted the kids, they suddenly went deaf and blind or found something besides their parents that required immediate attention.

I think it was their way of having a quiet vacation.

– *February 28, 1999*

Johnston family vacation, 1986

Finally, no need to drive my point home

The other day, Mrs. Johnston made me get out of my favorite position (lying in bed with the remote control in one hand and the newspaper in the other) and go out to the driveway to see something. While we were going through the house, Mrs. Johnston told me that our 18-year-old son purchased a car and he wanted to show it to us. "I don't want you to say anything negative about it," the Truly Unpleasant Mrs. Johnston hissed at me.

(I must digress a bit here. Mrs. Johnston is a mother, and therefore she loves her children unconditionally. They can do stupid things and she will still love them. She will just shake her head in wonderment at their stupidity and get on with raising them. On the other hand, I am a father, and while loving my children comes with the title to them, I think it is my duty to occasionally point out that the kids are nitwits. Mrs. Johnston feels that we don't have to point out anything. We just need to have total acceptance of every idiotic thing they do. These are our roles in life. With these points established, we can get on with the story.)

By the time we got to the driveway, Mrs. Johnston had gotten me to agree to be positive. No matter what, she warned. When I went around the corner of the garage and saw what was parked in our driveway, I let out a little groan. Have you ever seen that movie "Grapes of Wrath" with Henry Fonda? It's about the Depression and how Henry's whole family loads everything they own into an old jalopy and heads out for California and better times. If the Hollywood people were ever thinking about making an updated version of this movie, they should look up my 18-year-old son. He'd just purchased the car they would need to exude an authentic feel of desperation and poverty.

The first thing I noticed about the car was that it wasn't a car at all but one of those huge, truck-station wagon things that are about 6 feet off the ground. It was one of those vehicles you see in advertisements splashing through rivers, climbing cliffs and generally making pests out of themselves. This vehicle had gone through all that, and definitely looked worse for the wear. For one thing, the doors were a different color than the rest of the body, and even in the fading light, I could see spots of body rust.

And even through my sweatshirt, I could feel Mrs. Johnston pinching my arm. I didn't dare speak. Mrs. Johnston can pinch hard when she wants to make her point. Then the young lad popped the hood and let me get a look at the engine. The engine didn't seem like it was in any better shape than the rest of the truck, but I knew I had to say something or Mrs. Johnston was going to pinch my arm off.

"What kind of gas mileage does it get?" I asked innocently while looking at the greasy V-8 engine with a carburetor the size of a rain barrel.

"The guy said it gets about 17 miles to the gallon," the proud new owner said.

This beast would get 17 miles to the gallon coasting down Stevens Pass Highway in neutral, I thought to myself. Once you put your foot on the gas, the mileage would drop to 5 or 6 miles.

I continued to show amazing restraint when he started up the truck. Not only did the windows in our house shake from the noise, but the neighbors' windows were rattling, too. I couldn't wait to hear this rig pull into the driveway at 1 in the morning.

But an amazing thing happened. Our son drove it to work a couple of times — about 30 miles round trip — and apparently the noise made him deaf. And filling it with gas made him broke. Within a week, it was sitting in front of the house with a "For Sale" sign in it.

I didn't have to say a word. It's a sign the boy is growing up.

— November 4, 2001

Sticker shock of a higher degree

There used to be a time that when people talked about "sticker shock," they were talking about the price of a new car.

It seemed that people who hadn't purchased a new car in several years would be "shocked" to look at the sticker in the window and learn that a new car cost as much as their first house. Car sticker shock is the first type of shock for the average American.

Nowadays, we don't even blink when a friend tells us he just paid $19,000 for a new car. When they say they paid $150,000 for a house, we say, "Got yourself a fixer-upper, huh?" That's because most people already went through the second stage of sticker shock, known as buying a house.

Now there is a third stage of sticker shock looming just over the horizon for those of us who belong to what is considered the most important generation in the world: The Baby Boomers.

As a point man in the Baby Boomer generation (Class of '46), I can tell the troops there is a sticker shock coming up that will make taking a peek at the price of a new car look like taking the kids out for burgers on Friday night.

All it takes is a short talk with someone who goes by the title of "financial adviser." And all you have to do is mention that you are planning to send your kids to college, and are wondering how much you should be putting away.

"$400," the financial adviser tells you.

"$400?!" you repeat with a yelp. "I don't know if I can afford $400 a month."

"A month?" the financial adviser snorts. "I'm talking about a week."

"A week?!" you repeat. This conversation is beginning to sound like an echo chamber. The financial adviser says some incredibly insane thing, and you repeat it in a high shrill voice.

"Of course, that's if you want to send your child to Harvard," the financial adviser continues. "But there are institutions of higher learning that are less expensive."

"Less expensive?" your voice has dropped to a low babble.

"Why, of course," the financial adviser says. "You can always send your child to a state institution."

"State institution?" you obediently repeat, thinking only of Western State Mental Institution.

"Why, of course," this oily-tongued adviser continues. "There are several right here in the Puget Sound area. Why you could even send your child to somewhere out of the area, like Washington State University."

"Washington State University?" you mumble.

"Yes, I think with the proper money management, you can pay tuition and room and board by putting aside only $500 a month," says the financial adviser, whom you are beginning to dislike with each passing minute.

"$500 a month?!" you shout.

"I know that doesn't sound like much for a college education, but I think with your child being only 6 years old, it is the wisest course," the financial adviser says.

"Wisest course?" you mumble, thinking that it was a struggle just to save up enough money to pay for the hour with this adviser.

"Well, you could always purchase a small apartment house in the area where your child is attending college and hire your child as the apartment-house manager. Then you can pay the tuition as a salary and deduct it from your income tax. That way you can have an investment, and your child can have a job as an apartment-house manager."

"Apartment-house manager?" you repeat, thinking of a child who has a hard time remembering to get out of bed in time to go to the bathroom.

"Of course that would save on room and board, but it would require a down payment on the apartment house of about $200,000, and then the monthly payments ... "

About this time, the financial adviser glances up from the paperwork and notices you have fallen into a coma. Your mouth is hanging open.

"College sticker shock," the financial adviser says, and pats your hand. "There, there.

"You'll get used to it."

– September 20, 1992

At family reunion, we bask in togetherness

Every couple of years, the Truly Unpleasant Mrs. Johnston forces her immediate family (which means her husband and whichever children can't escape) into the mobile traveling torture chamber and we all drive to California.

Before readers start to think this is some kind of fun-filled family vacation where the Johnston brood gets to run on California beaches and shout things like "Surf's up!" these misguided readers should think of another adventure that also can be summed up in two words:

"Family reunion!"

Mrs. Johnston comes from a large Irish-Catholic family that has more people in it than some states. Some of these family members even have red hair and freckles to match in case there is any question about their Irish heritage.

Although I've never heard it said by any of these relatives, I know when they meet each other at the start of the day, they shout, "Top of the mornin' to you!" and do a little Irish jig.

But what they like to do most is get together every couple of years to see what everyone in the family has been up to. Where normal families would gather at one of the many ocean beaches in California so the children can swim and run on the sand while the adults sit around and drink, Mrs. Johnston's family likes to get together near Lake Tahoe.

Not at Lake Tahoe itself, but at a nearby site better known for another family gathering. This family reunion is known in history as the Donner party. Yes, Mrs. Johnston's family gets several cabins and rooms around the place where the Donner wagon train got stuck in the snow in the 1800s and that family passed the winter by eating folks who weren't related to them.

As far as I know, no one has been eaten at one of Mrs. Johnston's family reunions, but that doesn't mean it hasn't crossed their minds. I'm sure if we spent more than a week together there would at least be some snapping and biting on the non-family members — the people who married into the family, that is. We're known as the "out-laws," not the in-laws. We know where we stand.

As it is, a week seems about as long as Mrs. Johnston's family can stand each other. The first couple of days are spent saying how much they missed seeing the other family members and catching up on what has happened since the last reunion. By the third day, all the latest news has been shared and the clan starts talking about their childhoods. Mrs. Johnston's family grew up in an Irish-Catholic-overpopulated neighborhood south of San Francisco, and that leads to who did what to whom when they were children.

During these lively debates, I usually find another "out-law" who is on the sidelines of the family discussion, and we spend the evening trying to figure out some way to get back to our motel rooms. I told Mrs. Johnston I didn't think any of her family would miss me or any of the other out-laws if we slipped away, but she insists that we play an important role in the family reunions.

As far as I can tell that "important role" is to settle family disputes like who was the worst president of the United States (this is dangerous ground because as the family members grow older, they make more money and start moving from Democrat to Republican) or can public schools ever be as good as Catholic schools?

You can always tell the new out-laws in the group because they think someone in the family is actually interested in their opinions, and they open their mouths to say something stupid, such as what they think. Then the members of the family turn on these poor people and the rest of the out-laws watch the blood flow.

The older and more experienced out-laws have made a pact among themselves long ago. We are willing to sacrifice one of our own to draw attention away from the herd so we can live to another day.

After a few family reunions, these youngsters will learn this lesson and pass it on to the next generation of out-laws.

– November 10, 2002

Happily posing for a family portrait, 1987

Kids in sports means marathon for parents

Any parent with a child involved in sports had to be impressed with the Olympics in Atlanta.

The Truly Unpleasant Mrs. Johnston and I were watching one of those films about an American swimmer who, the announcer said, got up every day at 4 a.m. to go to a public swimming pool 75 miles away because there wasn't a public pool in his hometown.

Then the lad would go back 75 miles to be at school by 9 a.m. The routine would be repeated every day, and even on weekends, the announcer said in hushed tones. This went on for years, until he ended up in Atlanta in a skinny black bathing suit. He was about 15.

When Mrs. Johnston and I heard this, we turned to each other with our mouths hanging open in total admiration.

"That is one dedicated parent," we said.

After watching several of those short slice-of-life films, I concluded that behind every great athlete was a parent with 200,000 miles racked up on the family wagon hauling the kid to every practice and sporting event ever scheduled.

The Johnston children are involved in sports, and that means the Johnston parents are involved in sports.

Mom and Dad Johnston's main functions are providing a way for the children to get to the event, watching the event and then bringing the kids home after the event.

The other parent jobs are providing snacks for the team and standing on the sidelines pretending to be a goal post or local vegetation.

As the Johnston children grow older, the less we do or say the better, as far as they are concerned. Dressing like a chauffeur and pretending to work for the child would probably be perfect.

If the Olympics ever award gold medals to the parents who give the most to get their kids there, I think those with children in swimming should win every time.

The mother who hauled her son to the swimming pool 75 miles down and back earned our deepest respect. We have a daughter on a swim team and we know there is devotion to a swimming child that goes far beyond the usual sport.

When we told a friend that our daughter was on a swim team, she laughed in a disturbing way. A parent laughing and nodding with a smirk is not a good sign.

Some swim meets last all day and your child may be involved for only two races. One race may last 37 seconds and another for two minutes. The first race is scheduled for 8:37 in the morning, the other at 3:15 in the afternoon.

Some swim meets are held in outdoor pools in blazing sun. The more experienced parents bring tents. Other meets are held in covered pools and you get to sit in something like a chlorine sauna. Experienced parents bring gas masks.

One nice thing about swim meets is that parents can cheer their kids on and even offer loud advice. I don't think the kids can hear it underwater.

That may be the sport's attraction.

— *September 15, 1996*

Chapter 3

'Tis the season to be ... crazy?

...oh Christmas tree....

Illustration Copyright ©2010 by Paul Schmid

Unsafe and definitely insane

Next to Christmas, tomorrow is the favorite national holiday for the Johnston children.

Right after the kids finish ripping through their Christmas presents on Dec. 25 and complaining they didn't get what they wanted, they start planning how to make an end run around their mother, the Truly Unpleasant Mrs. Johnston, to get their eager sweaty hands on some fireworks for Fourth of July.

Of course, as responsible parents, we have banned all fireworks from our house.

Well, maybe not both of the Johnston parental units are that responsible and one parent has never said out loud he didn't want fireworks in the house. Matter of fact, there is one irresponsible parent who remembers his youth in Everett when his father showed him how to take two tin cans and put the smaller can inside the larger one, place a firecracker in a little hole in the top and blow the smaller can halfway to the moon…

And remembers the pleasures of spending a hot July afternoon putting firecrackers down the holes of an ant hill and pretending to be a construction crew building a superhighway so the ants can get to their jobs in the morning….

And the contests with the firecrackers where you tried to hold the firecracker after it was lit and throw it away before it exploded. Sometimes your timing could be a little off and the cracker would go off in your hand, leaving a blood blister the size and color of a grape and your fingertips ringing with electricity…

Or how about holding those tiny firecrackers called Lady Fingers in your hand and setting them off? While still holding them!!! Sure it stung, but it left a big impression on the other kids…

Or maybe taking those big red firecrackers with the fuse in the middle and going down to the 14th Street dock just across the railroad tracks, where you would tie a string together with a nail and the red firecrackers and throw them off the dock? These firecrackers would actually blow up underwater and sometimes a bullhead (a fish with an ugly expression) would come to the surface to check out what was going on topside…

Or how about flushing one down the toilet…

Oops, we can tell by the expression on Mrs. Johnston's face that she believes part of the firecracker problem in the Johnston household stems from my own fond memories of blowing up things in Everett to celebrate our country's independence.

Anyway, the children (at least the Johnston boys) start negotiating for fireworks right after Christmas and it works up to a full-time lobbying effort by June. They make the National Rifle Association look like a bunch of pikers

The kids start with the small stuff like Curly Snakes. These are little things that look like black rocks, and when you light them on fire, they start smoking and some kind of ash curls out of them. The kids like to dance around them while the rocks are smoking and curling. The children make loud whooping noises while doing this.

The Truly Unpleasant Mrs. Johnston doesn't like the curly things because:

1) They are burning.
2) They are smoking.
3) They leave burn marks on the sidewalk.
4) They need matches to get them going.

Anything involving matches and smoke is a hard sell at the Johnston house. Mrs. Johnston went to that Mother's School that taught that allowing children to light matches (other than for birthday cakes when they are old enough to drive and a candle at the church for some poor lost soul) would lead to children setting themselves on fire or, worse yet, setting the house on fire.

But if they can say "pleasepleaseplease" enough about the snakes, Mrs. Johnston will give in and say "OK, but just the snakes." Ha! What the children want is to get close to one of those firecracker stands where they will sell you a box of fireworks for the price of a new car. These are called "safe and sane" fireworks.

What the Johnston children really really REALLY want to do is get to the Indian reservation where they can get their sweaty hands on some "completely unsafe and completely insane" fireworks. The only way they will be able to do that is talk their irresponsible father into taking them.

– July 3, 1994

Seasonal fatigue sets in like clockwork

Right about now, everyone in the Johnston household is suffering from PCSS (Post Christmas Stress Shutdown), a common affliction where we get facial tics when we hear the first notes of "Jingle Bells" and my hands shake if one of the kids pulls the chain on that irritating battery-operated Santa Claus hanging on the door and he starts with that "Ho, ho, ho" noise.

PCSS has gotten so bad around here that there have even been times when I wanted to take down the Christmas decorations before New Year's Eve rather than keep them up until Valentine's Day. Some people might say I've lost the spirit, and I'm afraid the kids may be catching it from me.

It's hard to remember the year when I started to notice the first symptoms of PCSS. I do remember back in the early 1980s when I hit the couch a couple of days after Christmas and said out loud: "Boy, I'm glad that's over."

One of the kids popped his head out of a huge box that some toy came in (the toy itself broke several hours after the box was open, but the kids were more interested in playing in the box anyway) and looked at me like I lost my mind. The other kids stopped fighting over a toy that lost its name tag in the ripping-tearing-pulling part of Christmas-package opening that morning and now everyone claims the gift was meant for him/her.

Mrs. Johnston, who takes on the personality of Mrs. Santa Claus at this time of year, stopped baking cookies and humming happy seasonal songs in the kitchen and poked her head into the living room to say: "Oh, you don't mean that, Mister Stupid. You know you love Christmas."

My wife always claims to know what I like better than I know what I myself might like. "You know you love that Holiday Fruit Cake Jelly Roll Up," she will tell me when I remove a piece of the rock-hard stuff after it pulled out a couple of fillings.

Every part of my being may say I hate Holiday Fruit Cake Jelly Roll Ups, but because they start arriving in the mail around Thanksgiving (handmade by relatives with a grudge, I suspect) I am told I love them. Of course, I eat some just to prove that you can wash down anything with strong enough coffee.

Like the Holiday Fruit Cake Jelly Roll Up, I'm not allowed to say I hate Christmas. I know if I say that, then I will have to watch the video about the little boy who lost the Christmas spirit, but thanks to a friendly elf named Bob and an unlimited charge card, he was able to find the spirit again.

But in the last few years, I noticed that I started suffering from PCSS even BEFORE THE ACTUAL EVENT! I mean around the middle part of December, I start to mutter to myself about Christmas becoming a chore to celebrate. It's kind of like the advertisement for joining the Army: It's not a celebration. It's a job.

Because I actually live with Mrs. Santa Claus, I have to keep my feelings to myself. But it's stressful to be so cheerful for so long. The facial tics start around the 500th time I hear "Jingle Bells" and when the fourth or fifth Holiday Fruit Cake Jelly Roll Up comes into the house.

It's stressful on the kids, too. Not because they don't like Christmas. They love Christmas. What's stressful on the kids is trying to be good for so long. They know the casual smart-aleck remark that passes almost unnoticed during the summertime could wind up as a black mark against them on Santa's list. Or in this case, the muttering person known as Dad.

So they try to stay as well-behaved as they possibly can stomach and sneak around the house, hoping that one of the parents won't ask them to do something impossible like empty the garbage or even clean up their rooms. They know their usual comment of "I just did that last week" will earn the warning about Santa Claus watching them from a nearby fir tree and being uncooperative may cost them some little treasure come Christmas morning.

When Christmas does come and the kids find out they have been good enough to get only a new sweater and a book binder, they start suffering Post Christmas Stress Shutdown.

I can't wait to see how they will react to getting a Holiday Fruit Cake Jelly Roll Up next Christmas.

– December 27, 1992

Frightening changes – Halloween just doesn't get the kids' respect

As the Johnston children get older, they are giving up some old family traditions.

The kids say they are only wising up, but I view this as the further decline of the American family. After all, these traditions are what kept our family looking forward to those weird events that happen for no explainable reason every few months.

Of course, it helped that these family events included candy and money. Now the kids want the candy and money without going through the long – and the kids say drawn out – traditional part.

The first tradition that went out the window was the Tooth Fairy. Granted it was never a very believable story that a tiny person crept into their room at night and stole a bloody tooth from under the pillow and replaced it with a quarter.

But it was a family tradition that the kids followed faithfully and there were a few nights when the Truly Unpleasant Mrs. Johnston jumped out of bed, screaming that she needed a quarter to put under one of the kids' pillows.

Then she would come back to bed with the tooth. I never knew where she put those teeth and I never asked.

After a while, the Johnston children ran out of gullibility because they didn't talk about the Tooth Fairy anymore. They wanted cash up front for losing their teeth.

Next to go was the Easter Bunny. At first the kids loved looking for chocolate eggs and jelly beans. But as the years went by, they became more interested in the candy and less interested in hearing about the generous rabbit who came to the house late at night.

One of the most difficult characters to let go has been Santa Claus. The old guy wasn't hard for the kids to dump once they understood that didn't mean they would miss out on gifts, but Mrs. Johnston was sad to see him go. I think she still believes in him.

The toughest holiday for me to see the kids let go has been Halloween. When I was growing up in Everett, we enjoyed all the holidays but the excitement of a particular holiday only lasted a day or two.

Except Halloween.

A good Halloween could last through Christmas. If you planned it right you could still be enjoying Halloween right up till summer. The difference between Halloween and all the other holidays and family events is that the outcome is entirely in your hands.

The Tooth Fairy gave you a quarter and the Easter Bunny passed along chocolate eggs. Even at Christmas, you had very little control over the outcome. You got some cool stuff, but you also got a lot of underwear and sweaters.

But Halloween? You controlled that holiday. If you planned well (no houses with little old ladies passing out apples) you could fill a pillow case so full that you'd get a hernia hauling it home.

I planned my costume so it would be reversible. If I happened on a house that was giving out really good stuff, I could hit the house in my regular costume, go down the block, reverse the mask or wig, and go back for a second hit.

One of my cherished childhood memories is hitting one house for three cans of Coke. This was when rich people enjoyed canned sodas. The rest of us had Kool-Aid.

I retired from trick-or-treating when I hit my teens, but rediscovered the thrill of the full shopping bag of candy when my own children started hitting the streets on Oct. 31.

But when I asked the kids what they were dressing as for Halloween this year, they looked at me with a lack of enthusiasm. The older ones said they were going to parties and the younger ones thought they would go just around the neighborhood.

Small time, I thought. I wonder where my reversible costume is?

– October 20, 1996

Johnston children heading out for a night of trick or treating, 1989

Sure, it's the bunny everywhere else. But this is the Johnstons!

It's funny how family traditions get started. Take for instance the annual visit of the Easter Beagle.

Right now the Johnston family is pretty excited because there's less than a week to go before the Easter Beagle shows up to hide the hard-boiled eggs in the back yard. Johnston children are going to bed tonight with dreams of the Easter Beagle dancing through their heads. They can see him skipping around the yard, hiding a purple egg here and a yellow/green-striped, sick-looking egg over there.

Sure, there are some people right now who are saying to no one in particular: "The Easter Beagle?! Isn't it the Easter *Bunny* who hides the hard-boiled eggs around the yard?"

These people have their own strange family traditions and we have ours. After all, we live in Everett, where the other tradition is to climb the tombstone of the town's founder on Halloween and howl at the moon.

The annual visit by the Easter Beagle got started years ago when the Johnston clan started gathering at my brother Scott's house on Easter Sunday. There were a bunch of little kids, and the adults thought it would be fun to have an Easter egg hunt.

But someone had to hide the Easter eggs without drawing too much attention. It wouldn't look too good to see the adults out in the yard, crawling under bushes and hiding eggs in trees.

For some reason, Scott had a costume of a giant dog. I always felt it was left over from his troubled youth. It wasn't a giant dog costume that looked like Snoopy or even McGruff the Crime-Fighting Dog. It was a costume of a giant dog that looked as though it had been left outside for most of the year and needed a good bath and dry cleaning.

The costume was sort of white in places and sort of brown in other places. Or maybe it was just sort of a muddy color all over. That's the nice thing about family traditions. The actual memory of the event fades over the year until it becomes a big brown blur. The dog costume could have been orange for all I remember, but right now it seems to me that it's brown and white with big floppy ears.

The first year, Scott wore the Easter Beagle costume and he went around the yard, hiding hard-boiled eggs wherever he felt like it. If any of the kids happened to see him, we would explain that it was the Easter Beagle and he was filling in for the Easter Bunny, who was home with a cold. If any child went outside while the Easter Beagle was hiding the eggs, we told the kids, the Beagle may turn on them because we believed the Easter Beagle had rabies. Otherwise, how else could we explain the Beagle's color?

The kids bought the story because we're in Everett, where anything is possible.

When the Easter Beagle completed his task of hiding the eggs, he stood in the middle of the yard and gave the signal for the kids to start looking. It seemed to me there were always more kids waiting behind the line to look for eggs than there were children actually related to the different branches of the Johnston family.

There would be this mad dash across the lawn with the older kids heading straight for the bushes, trampling over the smaller ones. What is nice about having an Easter egg hunt with the family is that cousins don't feel bad about running over a littler cousin. It is almost like trampling on a younger sister or brother.

As the children were gaily tearing through the garden and breaking off tree branches looking for eggs, the other adults would stand to one side and say a silent prayer of thanks that this event was being held at Brother Scott's house and not theirs.

After the first exposure to the Easter Beagle, the kids started asking if the Easter Beagle was going to be there the next year. The next year, the original Easter Beagle refused to get into the costume, but there were older nephews who thought it would be cool to play the Beagle.

We discovered that cool feeling lasts only a time or two before the nephew discovers that the younger cousins think it's cool to do a flying tackle on the Easter Beagle in case he is holding out on the candy.

We've just about run out of older nephews, and the Easter Beagle may be passed down to the younger generation. Family traditions must be carried on, no matter how strange.

– March 27, 1994

The annual holiday photo, this one with a bunch of stony-faced people in Seattle's Fremont neighborhood, 1990

Stealth shopping: When it comes to Christmas gift-buying, nobody has it down like my wife

Like the department-store and shopping-mall magnates, the Truly Unpleasant Mrs. Johnston believes it is never too early to start thinking about Christmas. Although she has never said it out loud, I believe she starts planning for next year's Christmas right after the presents are opened for the Christmas we are celebrating at the moment.

When we were first married in the last century, she liked to set aside the entire month of December for Christmas planning. That included getting the Christmas tree, stringing the lights, decorating the house, buying presents for everyone she ever knew and getting mad at her husband because he is such a jerk for not getting into the Christmas spirit.

(I must digress a bit. During the first year or so of our married life, I was working like a dog just to put food on our table. I came home on Christmas Eve after slaving away, and I just wanted to rest. But Mrs.

Johnston said one of her 450 cousins was having a family hoedown in the foothills of Mount Pilchuck or somewhere, and she thought it would be a swell idea to drive several hours to attend this event.

(As I remember it, I told Mrs. Johnston that I worked all day and wouldn't it be nice if we spent Christmas Eve together, gazing into each other's eyes over a candlelit dinner. Mrs. Johnston remembers it slightly differently and claims I wanted to spend the evening lying on the couch, drinking beer and watching All-Star Holiday Wrestling.

(After all these years, I can't remember exactly who wanted to do what, but this incident taught me something important about married life. If you're married to a woman who thinks Christmas is *the* major holiday of the year, just go along with her or you are dead meat for 20 years or more.)

While I like to get into the Christmas spirit at about 5 p.m. on Christmas Eve by making a mad dash to the mall, I have reason to believe Mrs. Johnston does her Christmas shopping all year 'round. I can only guess at this because Mrs. Johnston doesn't believe in telling me anything that goes on around our house.

She says if I know what is going on, it might upset me. But months before Christmas last year, she came home with a tall glass flower vase. It was so tall that she couldn't smuggle it in the house, so I saw it and asked her about it. I figured it was just another tall glass flower vase for our house because I believe Mrs. Johnston's goal is to keep the tall-glass-flower-vase-makers in business.

So I was surprised when she said it was for one of her friends for Christmas. Because I'm not allowed to know what is going on in my own house, I have to put together clues dropped by Mrs. Johnston and the kids to get to the bottom of anything.

This is what I put together from this tiny clue: Mrs. Johnston bought a Christmas present for a friend in the middle of summer. Mrs. Johnston has dozens of such friends. If she bought this one friend a present, it stands to reason that she is planning on buying all her other friends, real and imagined, Christmas presents.

But because she is shopping in summer for Christmas presents, she is looking for good buys. And if she is shopping early for bargains, it means we are saving money.

When I told Mrs. Johnston that I appreciate her efforts to save money while at the same time satisfying her unnatural desire to shop, she looked at me and said: "Whatever you want to think is fine with me."

In other words, I still don't know what is going on.

—November 17, 2002

Chapter 4

Home Life: It's the pits

Illustration Copyright © 2010 Paul Schmid

Take cover: It is the zucchini wars!

Someone left a giant zucchini on my desk.

To anybody who doesn't live in the Seattle area or has just moved here from another planet, finding a zucchini on the office desk might be seen as a sign of friendship. "Why, what a thoughtful gift," this person might think.

I saw it differently. This was the opening shot in the 1990 Zucchini Wars.

As most people living in this area know, zucchini is the third most persistent vegetable matter on Earth, right behind morning glories and Seattle Times columnist Rick Anderson. Someone doesn't just "leave" a zucchini on your desk or back porch around here, any more than someone just "left" a horse's head in that guy's bed in "The Godfather."

No, this was a message, an unclear message but a message just the same. Attached to the zucchini was a note. It was made out of headlines cut out from the newspaper. The note said simply: "Eat Me."

What did that mean? Was it a threat, a dare or some kind of urban insult? It was hard to read what was meant behind those two words.

No, a person doesn't just give someone a zucchini without trying to send a message. It's like putting a dead fish on someone's desk in

61

Westport or a chicken on a desk in Lynden. Nobody is going to say, "Oh, boy, another chicken" when they find it on their desk. They are going to wonder what someone is trying to tell them.

Most people here don't need zucchinis. That's because anyone can grow zucchini. Even if your garden is just a wasteland of dead plants and morning glories, a zucchini plant will thrive. They love inattention.

Right now there are people all over the Seattle area looking out their back windows and saying, "Egad! There is a zucchini the size of a logging truck in our garden." The problem isn't growing them; it's what to do with them when they become big enough to live in.

I've known desperate people who have invited friends over for dinner, and while their guests were enjoying a meal of zucchini loaf, zucchini salad, zucchini bread covered with zucchini butter and topped off with zucchini chocolate cake, they were busy loading the back seat of the friends' car with zucchini.

No, when someone leaves a zucchini on your desk, you know this is a person who is on the edge. If they have gotten to the point of anonymously dropping off zucchini with the instructions "Eat Me," then this person was either sending out a cry for help or was already driven completely insane by zucchini overload.

Or they were declaring Zucchini War.

But it was too early in the year for Zucchini War to be declared. According to ZITS (Zucchini International Tribunal Society), Zucchini War can't be declared until all 1,238 recipes for zucchini have been used up, including the dreaded "Zucchini Abalone Surprise" and that holiday favorite: Zucchini Fruitcake. Once that was done – usually sometime in mid-October – a person could start the war, according to ZITS.

The rules of war are simple: Anything goes as long as the thing going is zucchini. You can leave them on doorsteps dressed up like babies, put them in handsomely wrapped Christmas packages, throw them into cars stopped at traffic lights or dress them up in little suits and send them to Washington, D.C., to serve in Congress.

But this zucchini appeared on my desk before the first week of September. I had gotten only through Zucchini Pancake Breakfast in my recipe book and hadn't even started on the brunch section when the zucchini appeared. This was a sneak attack and demanded quick action.

I wrapped up the zucchini in butcher paper, put it into a box and sent it to my relatives in California. I attached a note that said, "Washington State Official Goodwill Games Vegetable."

The war is on.

– September 16, 1990

Flipped over gadgets: Beware – they'll save you labor, but not trouble

I like to buy gadgets.

The Truly Unpleasant Mrs. Johnston doesn't call my purchases "gadgets." She likes to call them other things like "junk" or "waste of money" or even worse, "more junk that's a waste of money that will clutter up the house." In other words, Mrs. Johnston doesn't appreciate it if I bring home a labor-saving device that will make life easier for both her and me.

OK, maybe I had making things easier for Mrs. Johnston in mind when I brought home a mop that sprayed cleaner on the floor as you scrubbed, but she didn't have to show her lack of gratitude by putting the mop in the closet and refusing to use it. She said it left streaks, which I couldn't see.

(I must digress here. In the ongoing war of the sexes, Mrs. Johnston seems to be winning the battle where one spouse tries to make the other spouse feel guilty without actually saying anything. It's the case where actions speak louder than words. The labor-saving mop is a good example. For some reason, Mrs. Johnston thinks she should clean the kitchen floor by crawling around on her hands and knees with a wet dish towel. I didn't think this was the best way to clean the floor, and that's why I purchased the spraying-mop gadget.

(Some readers may think my purchase opened up a chance for me to take over the floor duty, and to that I say, "Don't be ridiculous!" Which means Mrs. Johnston gets to make me feel guilty while she wins extra points for doing something she knows I would never do. She pulled the same thing when she had all those children, knowing full well that I wasn't up to the task of birthing babies. I'm through digressing now, and will get back to labor-saving devices.)

Mrs. Johnston doesn't seem to mind when I buy a gadget for the workshop. That is apparently the one area where I don't have to explain what I bought or why I bought it. "This thing will hold the nail in place while I hammer it in," I tell Mrs. Johnston.

"Can't your fingers do the same thing?" she will ask, with one eye squinting at the gadget and the other glaring at my forehead. I don't know how she does this, but it always scares me.

"Well, sure," I tell her, "but this thing is all shiny and battery-operated. Besides, I might hit my fingers."

The other day I went to one of those huge department stores that have everything from underwear to truck tires. I was wandering through the aisles, mouth agape at the wonder of all the gadgets, when I came across a labor-saving device that I had seen advertised on a television commercial at 3 in the morning. It is called a Flip Fold, and what it does is fold your clothes so they stack up neatly in your closet. Now, who could pass on a labor-saving gadget like this? For only $7? I was sold.

But when I brought it home, Mrs. Johnston looked at it with the one eye squinting and said just two words: "One week."

Those people who have not, as I have, been married for the last two centuries might need an interpreter for those words. But the rest of us already know they meant that Mrs. Johnston thought I would use this new labor-saving folding device for one week, and then it would go in the closet.

As it turns out, the flipping gadget is great at folding T-shirts. But I hang my shirts and pants on hangers, so I don't need to flip and fold them. Unfortunately, I only wear a couple of T-shirts every week, and it takes about five seconds to flip and fold those.

Still, I take the flip-and-fold gadget out of the closet with a big production about how neat my T-shirts look all stacked on the shelves. Then I flip and fold. It takes longer to get the gadget out than to fold the T-shirts. But I plan to use it every week.

This is war — and I need the points.

– *August 10, 2003*

64

Who is that man in my bedroom?

Have you ever noticed when you have a contractor working on your house that after a few months the contractor and his crew just seem like a prolonged date?

Matter of fact, having someone work on your house is sort of like going out on a blind date. You don't know beans about this person (other than your mother saying, "Oh, you'll like him. He has a great personality and he knows drywall"), but you are going to be spending some time together.

A blind date may last only a few hours, but a good remodel job can last a few months. Whether a blind date or a remodel, you are putting your life on the line and hoping that this complete stranger entering your life isn't a complete maniac.

Even if the blind date turns out to be fairly sane, and you still don't get along, you always have the option of jumping out of the speeding car. But you can't just jump out of your house if your contractor turns out to be someone you wouldn't want to have a cup of coffee with, much less spend a few months passing in the hallway in your bathrobe.

You are stuck with this guy.

For one thing, by the time you discover you two are not going to get along and you think it's a good time to give this guy a firm handshake at the front door and bid him goodbye, your house is in pieces. Your roof is gone, your foundation cracked and you don't have a toilet.

Unlike a blind date, however, finding a contractor isn't as easy as saying to one of your friends or your mother that you would like to find someone for the dance Friday. People always have someone they are willing to line you up with. Good contractors are guarded as closely as good baby-sitters.

If someone knows a contractor who shows up on time, does the work on time, within the price first mentioned, and the house doesn't fall down when you close the front door, you are not going to let that guy's name get into the wrong hands. No more than you are going to give out the name of the baby-sitter who will show up on time, feed the kids, do the dishes and charge just $2 an hour.

Most people would rather disclose national secrets than give up those names.

The Johnston family has been lucky in getting contractors. Of course, like most males, I like to do the repair work myself until it gets to the point where whatever I am repairing is so hopelessly destroyed that the Totally Disgusted Mrs. Johnston yells something like: "If I see you pick up another hammer, I'm going to nail your feet to the floor."

Within a few months of making that statement, there is a guy in bib overalls and a tool belt wandering through our kitchen when I get up in the morning.

The blind date is on.

At first, meeting a new contractor is like starting any new date. You are on your best behavior when you meet. The Truly Unpleasant Mrs. Johnston cleans the house like the guy is going to move in. She tells me to put my socks and underwear in the laundry hamper rather than throwing them like a balled-up basketball at the hamper.

It doesn't do any good to say the contractor does the same thing at his home. "He's not at his home," Mrs. Johnston says. "He is at our home and I don't want him to think we keep dirty underwear on the floor."

As the date turns into weeks and it looks as though there is a future, we get to know each other's dance moves. We know when we hear the tool box bang open in the morning, it's time to clear out of the bedrooms. The contractor knows to walk heavy on the stairs when coming upstairs and to make throat-clearing sounds to give us a fair warning.

After a while, the contractor becomes one of the family. If we have a cake for dessert, the Ever Gracious Mrs. Johnston tells us to save some for the contractor. There is a pot of fresh coffee on the stove every morning.

Even Duke the Wonder Dog, who barks at the wind blowing through the trees, doesn't bark anymore when he hears the tool box being banged around in the basement.

Then one day, like any date, the contractor tells you it's all over. He shakes your hand at the door and says he'll call you.

He never calls.

– December 13, 1992

Dad and Tim at our backyard barbecue, 1990

Struck D.U.M.B.: It's a bad, bad time for the digitally impaired

Has this ever happened to you: You are talking to somebody on the telephone at work and they ask, "What is your home phone number?" And the only thing you can come up with is, "Duh?"

Maybe your home phone number is only seven digits or maybe the phone company screwed you up royally and gave you a new area code to remember, too. It doesn't matter because it is finally too many numbers for one brain to handle. Your brain shuts down.

You have been hit with D.U.M.B. (Digitally Undermined Memory Banks). You're lucky if you can remember your own name.

Of course, you try to cover up the fact that you forgot your own telephone number. The first couple of times it happened to me, I would chuckle a little and tell the caller something like: "I don't call my own home all that much" and then would make up some number that sounded like it could be mine.

If the person called it and found it was the wrong number, chances were better than even that the caller would think he or she wrote it down wrong and call me again at work to get the right number.

We would chuckle over their mistake and I would reassure them that the same thing has happened to me. This idle chitchat is designed to keep the other person occupied while I look around on my desk for my home phone number.

If I could get to another phone, my fingers would automatically dial my home number because they are programmed to hit the numbers in a certain pattern. I'm like a lab rat who has been taught to punch the red button if he wants lunch.

For example, I have been programmed to punch a series of numbers on the telephone pad in order to speak to the Truly Unpleasant Mrs. Johnston at home.

If they ever made a telephone with a different key-pad layout, my fingers won't do the walking in the right order. There's a good chance I would never speak to Mrs. Johnston again. At least, not on a telephone.

Once again, I would have been struck D.U.M.B.

The problem is that there are too many numbers to remember and there is only so much space inside your head for storing them. There are telephone numbers for home and office plus phone numbers for a spouse's office. You might have a car phone (and what red-blooded, gadget-crazed American doesn't?), plus maybe a beeper.

And these are just the phone numbers. How about withdrawing cash from the bank? If you use the phone, there is a 10-digit number to start the banking process, and then your secret number to get money moved around.

The banks tell you to not use a secret number that might be convenient to remember, such as your birthday or address. "If you can remember it," the bank people warn, "then someone else might guess it."

So you give yourself a secret number that you can't remember. This is in case a crook gets your bank card and tortures you until you confess you can't remember the secret number.

The other day I stopped at the supermarket and wanted to use my bank card to pay. The machine asked for my secret code, which

I remember the same way I remember my home phone number: like a chicken pecking at buttons for corn (left top, drop down one, back to top row). But the grocery store had changed key pads and I stood there feeling as though I was being caught shoplifting as I poked at the numbers.

The cashier watched. People behind me watched. I punched away at the keys until I had to confess I had been struck D.U.M.B. I finally had to pay cash.

I am still embarrassed about the incident, but I figure by next week I'll forget it, because those brain cells will be filled with something else.

– October 4, 1998

Here, boy! Good boy!
(Who is *really* on the end of the leash?)

Anyone who lives with a dog wasn't surprised when researchers discovered that dogs could understand what people were saying to them, could figure out what object we were talking about when we told them to "get the red rubber ball," and were smarter than most people.

One researcher said his dog understood more than 200 words, and when he told the pooch to do something, the dog just did it without looking at him like he'd lost his mind.

I've had dogs all my life. Most have been black labs because they are friendly and generally can tolerate humans better than other dogs. The most tricks any of these dogs have been able to do is sit and shake hands. If I threw a ball and told them to "fetch," they all looked at me like I'd lost my mind.

"You just had the ball and then you threw it away," the dogs seemed to say. "Now you want me to run across the street, pick up the ball and bring it back so you can do it all over again? How about bringing me another treat, and we'll call it a day?"

(I must digress for a moment. While I've never asked much of the Johnston children, I have asked them to occasionally help around the house. I figure I've been providing them room and board, so the least they can do is take out the garbage and pick up their dirty clothes.

69

I've also provided room and board for the dogs, but I can't think of one thing I've ever asked them to do — and that includes cleaning up after themselves.

Now who do you think is the smartest?)

Dog people know their dogs can understand English or whatever language they happen to speak. They can even spell words. But it doesn't stop there.

When the Truly Unpleasant Mrs. Johnston and I would take our labs for a walk, one of us would say something reckless like "Let's go for a walk," and get the leash. As soon as the dog heard the word "walk," he would come bouncing to the front door and generally make a pest out of himself until we were out the door.

None of the dogs understood about having to put on jackets or shoes. We said "walk," and they were dressed and ready to go. So we stopped saying "walk" when we were getting ready to go out for a walk. Instead, we started to spell W-A-L-K. But the crafty dog somehow knew how to spell and rushed to the door, bouncing and ready to go.

We stopped talking and spelling with our current canine, Rex the Wonder Dog, because he understood *everything*. It was like having a spy living in the house. Mrs. Johnston and I were reduced to signaling each other with rapid eye movements that it would be nice to go outside for a walk.

We'd pretend to be going into the front room but would grab the leash and head out the front door. A bouncing, overjoyed dog was already there, waiting to begin his adventure. I think he could sense the change in our body temperature and know something was up.

In the past couple of months, I've become convinced that the dog has started to read my mind — or maybe do something to me with his mind that forces me to do his bidding.

Right now, Rex is sitting on our bed and watching me closely. Each time I type in the word "walk" he sits up and stares at me. Watch this: WALK!

I have to sign off now. The dog and I are going for W-A . . .

– *August 29, 2004*

70

Just scraping by? In making sandwiches, perhaps even the rich can relate

The other day I was making a peanut-butter-and-jelly sandwich and I started thinking about Bill Gates.

The reason I started thinking about Bill Gates was because the peanut-butter jar was almost empty. There was maybe enough peanut butter left inside to cover a tiny corner of the bread. But to get that tiny bit of peanut butter would require some scraping with the bread knife.

So I'm standing in the kitchen with a knife in one hand and a family-size jar of creamy-style nearly empty peanut butter in the other hand. And I'm thinking: What would Bill Gates do?

I don't mean would Bill Gates invent a robot that scrapes out the last bit of peanut butter from the jar. But would Bill Gates take the time to insert the bread knife into the family-size jar of peanut butter and get the last tiny remains before putting the jar in the sink to be washed out for recycling? I'm assuming that Bill recycles, but I don't know about scraping.

Bill Gates happened to meander through my thoughts at that moment because there was a news story about him being the richest man in the world. He had almost $50 billion. The amount was down some from past years, but still, it was a sizable chunk of change.

So I'm thinking the guy has almost $50 billion, making him the richest guy in the world, but he eats at the same places I eat (a drive-in hamburger place in Bellevue and Dick's next to the Seattle Center, for crying out loud!), and I like to think of him as a neighbor (he lives a couple miles from me, as the crow flies). And I'll bet his wife tells him that he shouldn't be eating those hamburgers from the fast-food places just like the Truly Unpleasant Mrs. Johnston tells me.

I don't know if Bill Gates likes peanut-butter-and-jelly sandwiches, but if he does and he comes to the last scrapes of peanut butter, does he take the time to dig it out or does he throw the jar away?

Or when he takes a shower in that fancy-pants mansion on Lake Washington (I cannot imagine Bill Gates wasting the time to take a bath, nor do I want to have that image in my head), I wonder if he turns the shampoo bottle upside down so he can get the last few drops out of the bottle before throwing it away.

When you are the richest person in the world, you can hire people to scrape out your peanut-butter jars and to turn your shampoo bottles upside down, but that might go against the grain of a guy who buys hamburgers at Dick's. It certainly goes against my grain.

Bill Gates and I are about the same age (102 years old, according to our children) and were raised by parents who lived through the Great Depression and World War II, so they knew tough times, and life was not always easy, and material things could disappear in a flash. That includes peanut butter and shampoo.

While it may be true that my neighbor Bill Gates may have a thicker cushion against the problems of the world than most of us, some things from your upbringing stick to your mind like creamy peanut butter. And I'm sure that Bill Gates' mother said to him at some time: "Bill, waste not, want not." I know my mother did, and I like to think mothers still say things like that to their children.

After I scraped out the last bit of peanut butter and started eating my sandwich, I asked Mrs. Johnston if she thought Bill Gates scraped the jar, too.

"I'm sure he does," she said without missing a beat, "and those sandwiches are bad for him, too."

I also like to think that's something Bill and I have in common. Wives who like to remind us we would be dead if they didn't watch us like hawks.

– April 4, 2004

Barrett and Dad celebrating Christmas in California, 1985

Turbo-charged dreamer

When I was asked what I wanted for Christmas this past season, I said that was easy. I believe I speak for the majority of American males by saying I wanted a gasoline-powered, turbo-charged can opener.

Fat lot of good it did me.

Despite the growing demand for a gasoline-powered, turbo-charged can opener — and the untapped market it represents — no one has yet invented this labor-saving gadget.

That loss, of course, is a gain for women who are married to or involved with the American male who, upon hearing that such a can opener existed, would march down to the mega-hardware store and demand one. These males would promptly have to go on a waiting list, because such a device would be sold out before it even got on the shelf.

I happened to think about the need for this kind of can opener the other day when the can opener I purchased three years ago gave up the ghost. This wasn't a gasoline-powered, turbo-charged unit, but it wasn't an ordinary can opener, either.

This scientific marvel could open cans — tall ones, short ones, fat ones and skinny ones — but it could also sharpen knives and scissors, seal plastic bags, open bottles of beer, remove lids and cut through those pesky plastic bags with the skill of a heart surgeon.

When I brought home this modern miracle, the Truly Unpleasant Mrs. Johnston had only one question for me. No, it wasn't her usual "have-you-lost-your-mind" question, either.

"Will that thing open a can of soup?" Mrs. Johnston asked, giving the modern miracle her squinty fish eye.

Up to this point in our marriage, Mrs. Johnston had opened cans with some crude device she held in her hand! She would put the can in one hand, line it up with the opener, then she would turn a knob to make it operate. I told her that was like doing the laundry by pounding it on the rocks by a river.

"What we have here," I said, holding the electric can opener, "is the answer to all those wasted minutes and sprained thumbs from turning that knob. No longer will cans of beans be spilled across the counter because they slipped out of the old-fashioned can opener. This baby will not only open the can for you, but it will also hold it in place and even remove the lid. You'll never cut your fingers again."

"I never cut my fingers. That was you," she said. "We'll see how this works."

(I must digress here. I love gadgets. If it plugs in, turns on or fires up, I'll buy it. Or if it has the description "labor-saving" anywhere on it, I'll buy it.

(One time I bought a gadget that looked like a hammer but had three different screwdrivers in its handle. When I showed Mrs. Johnston this wonderful labor-saving tool, she asked me if it wouldn't have been easier to just get a hammer or screwdriver I already had out in the garage.

(Ha! I wanted to say. That's the trouble with women. They don't see the big picture. With a lack of vision like that, I wanted to say, we would have never had the flat-screen television or the remote control. Of course I didn't say anything, but I think you see my point. I am through digressing now and will continue.)

74

Unfortunately, the electric can opener failed to live up to its promise. Maybe it would have, but the instructions were so long and boring that I lost interest before getting to the part on how it worked. I used my time-honored approach to figuring how something worked by playing with it and trying different things.

That goes on until the thing breaks and I have to buy another one. But my dream opener is not invented yet, and that party-pooper Mrs. Johnston bought a new opener.

It's electric, but all it does is open cans!

– December 5, 2004

Wisdom through the ages

The other day I was talking to my kids on my favorite subject entitled "When I was younger." These are usually one-sided conversations where I talk and the kids try to look interested while thinking of some way to escape.

This particular conversation was about the price of homes around Seattle. I had just received my home appraisal from King County, and I said I was thankful we weren't shopping for a home now because we couldn't afford to buy one. "When your mother and I bought our first house," I told the glassy-eyed children, "they were less expensive than what I just paid for our new car."

"Oh, Dad," one of the children squealed, "you bought that house when you came to Seattle with the Donner party."

One thing you can say about the Johnston children is that they aren't historians, but they are amusing in their confusion. I was going to point out that the Donner party became trapped in the mountains near California in the 1800s and ate each other to survive. Apparently this child confused the Donner party with the Denny party, which came to Seattle in the 1800s and settled in. They later became stars of a television show called "Here Come The Brides." As far as anyone knows, the Denny party didn't eat anyone.

The point I was trying to make with the children was that it didn't always cost a half-million to buy a house in Seattle. My first house cost $26,000, and I didn't buy it in the 1880s or during the Depression. I

75

bought the house in 1974. When I sold that house in 1980 for $85,000, I thought it was a fair price. I used the money to buy another Seattle fixer for $87,000. It had more bedrooms because the Truly Unpleasant Mrs. Johnston and I had doubled the size of our family from two children to four.

Now, that may be surprising to some people but here is something I would call really surprising. That $26,000 house just sold for $525,000! And it doesn't even have off-street parking. You parked on the street and walked up two flights of stairs to get to the front door. The other day, one of our old neighbors said he heard the house I bought for $85,000 was going on the market for $1 million. I would have done a double-take if someone told me that two years ago. Now I think the guy is asking too little. He could go for $1.25 million.

There are a couple things that are scary about today's home prices. First, the business market can turn bad quickly. No jobs means no money, and you can't carry $4,000-a-month house payments if you are collecting unemployment. When I came to Seattle in the late 1960s, Boeing had just laid off 100,000 or more workers, and people were walking away from their homes. The newspapers were filled with house ads, and, finally, the government had to sell these homes for whatever was owed on the mortgage. There were five-bedroom homes near Volunteer Park going for under $40,000. Some of my friends bought their homes for $30,000, raised their families and are ready to make a big chunk of change when they sell their homes.

I can't sell my home at the moment. I still have one kid in college and one is still living with us. At the price of homes around here, these kids will be living with us for years to come. One just graduated from college, and he is looking at jobs that pay under 10 bucks an hour. Maybe he can afford $700 a month for an apartment, but it will be years before he can afford a house.

Like most parents, I like to share the wisdom I have collected over the years. My father used to do the same thing when I was a kid. Of course, I ignored him. But years later, something my father told me would pop into my head, and it was always good advice. Maybe something I say now to my kids will pop into their heads 20 years from now.

I have told the kids that I am "land rich but cash poor." One day they will be paying their mortgage and they will call me. "Dad, do you remember when you told me that you were land rich?"

– March 19, 2006

The party line: The old still talk; the young just text

I like to read gossip columns about the lives of rich and famous people. They are usually about some stupid thing these folks said or did, something I probably would do, too, if I were rich or famous.

The other day I read that a well-known movie actor married a woman who was 23 years old. While this marriage may be a happy and long-lasting one, what got my attention was that this particular groom was my age.

"I have pants that are older than this guy's bride," I say to the Truly Unpleasant Mrs. Johnston.

"Not to mention your underwear," Mrs. Johnston replies.

Despite what my children may think, I am not older than rock formations in the Cascade Mountains. When I mention the Civil War, it doesn't mean I witnessed it firsthand. The same is true about World Wars I and II, but these events get mixed up in younger people's head and they are lumped in with events like Vietnam (which I did have a role in) and most things that happened before MTV.

In other words, if it happened before 1990, the kids consider it ancient history.

While the idea of marrying a woman younger than some of my pants has some appeal — for instance I would have a new audience for my jokes, and I would require her to call me "Mr. Johnston" — I wouldn't like the idea of having someone around who, when I said something about Richard Nixon, would need me to explain who Richard Nixon was.

That's one of the benefits of being married to the same person for more than a quarter of a century. It saves a lot of explaining. And when you mix in most of your friends having the same lengthy marriages, you can hold a whole conversation just in a few words.

"Nixon."

"Watergate."

"Bad."

The other day I was talking with my college-age daughter and her friends. The young ladies all had these new portable telephones that not only make phone calls (which is what a telephone is designed to do) but also allow you to send typed messages to another telephone (called "text messaging"). You can even send photographs that you have just taken with the same telephone.

This is just short of being amazing, but our children take it for granted. I wanted to tell the kids how amazing I thought these telephones were and started to tell a story from my youth. This is something the Johnston children are always eager to hear. ("Oh boy, Dad is telling a story from his youth in Everett," they scream as they gather at my feet . . . Oops, sorry. I was hallucinating.)

"When I was a kid," I began, "we used to have party lines."

"We still have party lines," a child said. "You want to have a party, all you have to do is text message your phone list that you are having a party."

"No," I said, chuckling the way old folks do when they want to let the other person know they lost their minds, "each house in your block was connected to the same phone line, and when a phone call was for you, it would ring a certain way. Your ring might be two long rings and a short while your neighbor's might be two shorts and a long."

"You mean, you had to answer the phone at your neighbor's house?" a child asked.

"No, you had your own phone in the kitchen. But you couldn't use it if someone else was on the party line."

By that point, I had talked more than 30 seconds, which is beyond the MTV children's allotted attention span, so they turned back to text messaging and sending pictures of their father looking like a goofball.

I told Mrs. Johnston that it was better to be married to her than to a 23-year-old. Mrs. Johnston looked over at me and said, "Some 23-year-old out there is very thankful for that."

— October 31, 2004

Hey, is that weed laughing at me?

A couple of Mays ago, I decided to plant tomatoes in a little flat piece of land I managed to win back from the morning glories.

It seems like May is the time of year when you want to crawl around in your backyard like some kind of dog, scratch at the earth and plant something. I wanted to plant tomatoes.

I don't want to give away any gardening secrets, but you can purchase tomato plants that are almost all grown up from the neighborhood hardware store. You can get jumbo tomato plants that come in their own junior garbage cans.

I bought the jumbo plants because I figured I needed a jump on getting these things going. Each one cost $1.69 and I purchased six of them. To give you an idea how they would look after they became all grown up, the junior garbage cans had pictures of the tomatoes plants pasted on the sides.

The plants were as tall as a tree and the tomatoes were the size of bowling balls.

The clerk told me that maybe I would like some kind of wire frame to hold up the plants. When tomatoes get to be the size of bowling balls, I was told, the plants fall over. I bought six of them at $1.99 each for the flat spot where I cleared out the morning glories.

The clerk said I also needed tomato plant food, some slug bait and a little tool that looked like the center part of a toilet paper roll, but with a handle on one end. You use this to dig a hole to put the tomato plant in, the clerk said. The food, slug bait and toilet-paper thing came to $12. Add in the rest of the stuff, and the bill came to over $33, or a little over five bucks per tomato plant.

It's a funny thing about tomato plants. They may look like little trees, but when they fall over in the trunk of your car while bringing them home from the hardware store, their little arms break in half.

So when I arrived back home with my six tomato plants in their junior garbage cans, they had been reduced to four healthy ones and two wounded in action. I figured even with half of the limbs left, I would still have enough tomatoes to supply the Johnstons with BLTs for the year.

After I planted the tomatoes in my scratched-out piece of hardpan and put the wire cages around them, I figured I did my part. But Mrs.

Johnston, who figures she knows everything, said my work had just begun. According to her, it requires more than planting tomatoes to get a crop the size of bowling balls.

"You are going to have to weed and water them," the Truly Unpleasant Mrs. Johnston said with that tone people who actually plant things use to talk with the rest of us.

As it turned out, I didn't have to do any of that weeding and watering stuff. It was a typical Seattle May. I planted in the hot sunshine and the next day it rained. It rained through the week and then the sun came out for a day and then it rained again and then the sun came out. Every time I started to think about looking in on my tomato plants, it started to rain.

Finally, I was able to get out to the garden. Anyone who has lived in the Northwest for more than a year knows what happens when it rains and then the sun comes out and then it rains and so on. Morning glories (or better known by their Latin name: Plantus From Hell) spring up.

The morning glory vines had wrapped themselves around the necks of the tomato plants that weren't killed in the car ride home and strangled them. The amazing thing about this is that Mrs. Johnston never said "I told you so" once.

I got one tomato out of the six plants. It was the size of a golf ball and cost $33. Or $400 a pound.

Last winter, a 5-pound bag of potatoes went bad under the kitchen sink and I was going to throw it out. Instead I cut some spuds in half and put them in the holes where I had pulled out the tomato plants. I forgot about the potatoes until end of summer when Mrs. Johnston said it looked like I had a crop.

We had them for dinner that night. Couple of days later, I dug up some more and made potato salad. There was no cost.

This should make me happy, but the other day I went to check on the garden for spring planting and the potato plants were starting to grow again. Next to them the morning glories were growing. They seemed to be getting along.

But I think I heard them laughing.

– May 23, 1994

80

You call that a pool?
I call it a swamp of work

This time of year I can't help but remember the day I thought I was making the smartest move of my life.

We were thinking of buying a house, and it had no yard. When those few sunny days in Seattle rolled around, I thought, I wouldn't have to start the endless mowing, trimming, whacking, weeding and everything else that goes with having a yard.

What this house *did* have was a swimming pool. Instead of grass, I'd have 33,000 gallons of water encased in cement right outside my back door.

The pool was a selling point. I actually had thoughts of our four kids swimming and playing in it when they weren't beating on each other.

A hot tub is built into this pool, and I pictured the Truly Unpleasant Mrs. Johnston and I sitting in the tub on warm summer nights, clicking our wine glasses together and enjoying a full moon. After getting too hot, we could roll over into the pool and cool off with a few laps.

But something happened between the time I bought the house with the pool and the end of the first year we lived in the house. That something is called *reality*.

Next to having children, the most labor-intensive thing a couple can do together is buy a house with a swimming pool. Like a child, a swimming pool requires constant monitoring. You have to take its temperature, and when the temperature goes up, you have to start adding chemicals so it doesn't get sick.

But unlike a child, a swimming pool must be fed "medicine" around the clock. I have a garage full of chemicals to keep the pool feeling good. At least with the kids, I don't have to feed them chemicals every day to keep them feeling good.

The first few years with the pool went pretty well. The kids were in it every day. I liked to have a few laps after work, and we used the hot tub on the weekends. But our kids grew up and started their own lives. While the kids were becoming less dependent on Mom and Dad, the pool didn't change in its demands. The water still needed to be balanced, the giant filter had to be cleaned and the leaves had to be skimmed off.

I started putting a cover over the pool earlier in the year so I didn't have to clean out the leaves and worry about stuff blowing into the pool.

One year I decided to leave the cover off, but that stunt left it exposed to the elements, and the pool caught a bad cold. Another year I found out it was just as dumb to leave the pool uncovered for more than a couple weeks. When I went to clean off the leaves I found out I had created what looked like a chemical experiment gone bad. The pool water was almost black, and the more I skimmed off the scum on top, the worse it looked.

When I fished out as many floating things as I could, I called the pool man and told him I had a chemical experiment growing in my yard. He chuckled the way people chuckle when they are going to take you to the cleaners. Sort of like the chuckle your mechanic gives when you tell him that you were running the last few days with the red light glowing in your dashboard.

After the pool man gave me an estimate, I told my three sons that it was time they paid me back for the room and board. It took almost the whole summer to empty, clean and fill the pool. You cannot appreciate how much water is in 33,000 gallons until you have to drain it all out and then fill it from a garden hose.

Now I keep the pool covered with a huge blue tarp. You can probably see it when you are flying into SeaTac.

While our kids have moved on, I can't say the same for the pool. I looked into filling it with dirt and turning it into a garden, but that's not allowed. Something about the water table. Before filling it in, you have to get a jackhammer and break the pool into tiny pieces.

I guess I will keep "the cement pond" in the backyard. But now I can understand why the guy I bought the house from just chuckled when I saw the pool and said to him, "I never had a house with a pool. It looks like fun."

When we sell the house, I will also try not to smile too much when the new owner says he always wanted a swimming pool.

– June 10, 2007

Chapter 5
Life in hell (not really, dear!)

Peering into glass houses is revealing: Where are all the rich people?

Mrs. Johnston likes to take our dog for a walk after supper. Unfortunately, she insists I go with her.

Usually we walk around our neighborhood. We exchange greetings with the neighbors who are outside and wave at the ones we see moving around inside their homes. Because our dog likes to run after other dogs and anything else moving, Mrs. Johnston keeps him on a leash. She also keeps an eye on me in case I try to make a break for freedom.

Every now and then, to change the routine, the Truly Unpleasant Mrs. Johnston will have us drive to a different location for the walk. She usually picks a neighborhood near the water. This means we are walking in a neighborhood with houses on the lake.

These are very expensive homes. Property that common folk like me cannot even afford to make the down payment on, so the monthly mortgage on these mansions is out of the question.

(I must digress. I bought my first house in Seattle in 1974. I paid less for this house than I paid for a car I bought last year. I sold the house for four times the purchase price and used the money to buy another Seattle home.

(We sold that house also for four times what we originally paid for it, and we bought a home in Bellevue. Bellevue is a fancy-pants address to have — some folks call it "Swellvue" — and there are expensive homes around here. I'm talking about homes that sell in the seven- and eight-figure range.

(These rich folks live either on the edge of Lake Washington — think Bill Gates — or on top of one of the hills that loom over the hovels for peasants like us. Don't get me wrong. We have a lovely home, but it wouldn't qualify as a tool shed in some of the high-priced neighborhoods around Swellvue. I'm through digressing now, and will get to my point.)

Mrs. Johnston decided she wanted to walk Rex the Wonder Dog and her husband through a fancy-pants neighborhood where people not only enjoy a view of Lake Washington but also have large boats tied up to docks in their front yards.

While Mrs. Johnston was impressed with the gardens in the front yards and the lovely stained-glass windows, I noticed something that, frankly, I found disturbing.

It was about 7 o'clock on a warm evening, but there were no people around. I'm not saying there were no people in the yards of these fancy-pants homes playing ball with the kids.

There were no people outside or inside!

The big homes had lots of glass so you could look right through to get a peek at the lake. But I never saw one human being walking around inside. No one was making dinner and no one was reading or watching television like regular folks. Maybe there was a light on in a hallway or two, but the rest of these mansions were dark and empty.

I asked Mrs. Johnston if she didn't find it odd there were no humans in sight. I didn't even hear the occasional dog barking at us as we went by. When Mrs. Johnston said the people were probably still at work, I said I didn't think so.

"I think they are inside those fancy-pants homes," I said, "but I think they are actually robots who work for all these computer companies around here. I think when they come home, they go into a closet and plug themselves in so they can recharge for the next day."

"I think I'm ready to put you in a home," Mrs. Johnston said, "where no one will see you again."

I decided not to continue this line of reasoning but I think most people will agree about rich folks being robots.

– October 26, 2003

How my Christmas gift-buying story turned into a soap opera

After being married to the Truly Unpleasant Mrs. Johnston for two centuries, I have to admit that I have run out of ideas on what to buy her for Christmas.

When we were first married in the last century, it wasn't very hard to buy her stuff. One Christmas I could get her jewelry and the next Christmas I could get her a nice 16-speed blender. That way I would learn that Mrs. Johnston didn't consider a kitchen appliance an appropriate Christmas gift. So the next Christmas I would get her a sweater made from the hand-spun wool of yaks, which she liked, so I figured I was safe in buying her clothing.

But the next Christmas I would give her a red teddy nightgown with white nylon fur, which she didn't like even though it could be loosely called "clothing." I was back to guessing again.

By the end of this past century, I had pretty well moved my gift-buying through every room in the house. I had eliminated most items for the kitchen as gifts, unless they were absolutely worthless and cost a lot, and items for the bedroom were not received well, especially if there was a chance I might enjoy them more than Mrs. Johnston.

There was a time I completely lost my mind and went to Costco to buy a 50-gallon barrel of laundry detergent, and I learned that most women don't see the good intentions behind such a gift. Some don't even see the good-natured humor behind a barrel of detergent.

(I must digress here. Over the years, Mrs. Johnston has lost her sense of humor altogether when it comes to gift-buying. When we were first married, she described most things I bought as "cute." Then, as the years wore on, she started calling them "barely tolerable." I think in the last few years "justifiable homicide" has been her favorite thing to mutter when she unwraps a gift.

87

(In any case, the whole arrangement has me completely mystified. It's so different from the way we men operate. If there is something I really want, I do what most guys do: I buy it. After all, if you need a drill, you probably need it RIGHT NOW! So you buy it and drill the holes. But if you can wait several months for Christmas to get it, then you probably don't really need it all that bad and you can wait for the sale to buy it. When I told Mrs. Johnston about my philosophy on gift-buying, she said I was an idiot and she hopes her next husband doesn't think that way. I am through digressing now.)

As we have moved into the second century of our marriage, I've found myself dreading Christmas. Besides the fact it costs a lot of money and seems to put Mrs. Johnston on edge, it also hurts my head thinking about it.

For example, when I ask Mrs. Johnston what she would like for Christmas these days, she tells me to "surprise" her. That can mean anything, and over the past two centuries, I have found that when I really do "surprise" her, Mrs. Johnston is more disgusted than delighted.

And if I told Mrs. Johnston to "surprise" me for Christmas, I would have to sleep with one eye open just in case she thought a big surprise would involve creeping up on me with a baseball bat while I was napping.

But I think I've come up with a fabulous surprise gift for Mrs. Johnston: I will get one of those 50-gallon barrels of laundry detergent, but this time I'll stuff a package of thong underwear in the middle of it.

Mrs. Johnston will first be disappointed that I bought her the same gift (laundry detergent) as I did a few years ago, but then she will be absolutely knocked out of her socks when she comes across the thong underwear around July.

I expect her to have a big surprise for me, too. I just hope it doesn't involve a baseball bat.

— December 8, 2002

Marriage by the book, from whispering sweet nothings to muttering sneaky somethings

When you get married, you are like an explorer in uncharted territory. Sometimes the natives are friendly and sometimes they seem to be hostile and capable of caving in your head with a baseball bat.

I look at my quarter-of-a-century marriage to the Truly Unpleasant Mrs. Johnston as a daily adventure. Each day I wake up, feel for all my vital parts and, if none is missing, begin my day's new adventure. I know there will be surprises in store because Mrs. Johnston insists on keeping me on my toes.

"If you're not on your toes," Mrs. Johnston likes to say, "you may get run over by an SUV loaded with kids heading to soccer practice!"

In the past few years, Mrs. Johnston has taken up muttering. This has made my life a living hell because I cannot find anywhere that addresses "Muttering" in the "Wife Manual" that I was issued after our wedding.

The "Wife Manual" seems to start after you've been married 20 years or more, so maybe the editors don't think it is necessary because you should be used to each other by then.

The truth is, you are still exploring this new and hostile real estate, and any guidance you can get would be helpful. But maybe "Muttering" is in Mrs. Johnston's "Husband Manual" under the general category of "Ways to Confuse Your Mate."

In this section, it would tell the woman to establish guidelines at the beginning of the marriage where a husband is expected to listen to whatever you have to say. If the male's attention drifts away — say, after 20 to 30 seconds of nonstop talking — the wife is supposed to ask, "ARE YOU LISTENING TO ME?!"

After she frightens the male into thinking she is actually insane and may harm him when he isn't paying attention, the female is instructed to change tactics.

"After the 15th year of marriage," the manual advises, "you may start addressing the cat or dog in the same tone of voice that you use when addressing the male. This will cause the male to believe you are telling him not to drink out of the toilet or asking him if he wants a bone to chew on.

"The male will relax and think you have given up talking to him. He will get back to doing something like reading the newspaper or watching TV. Now is the time to strike! Approach the male with a simple question, such as, 'Did you pick up the dry cleaning like I asked this morning?'

"Watch for the panic in his eyes. He may start to stammer. He may say something like, 'You didn't say anything about it this morning.' Just nod your head and look disappointed. Now you are ready for the next chapter:

" 'Muttering: The Attraction of Distraction.' This chapter will show you how to talk to yourself while letting both the dog and spouse believe you are talking to them."

The reason I happen to know about this ploy is because I overheard a conversation between Mrs. Johnston and her female friends. You know how women invite couples over for dinner and the men go into one room and the women go into the kitchen?

Well, the women are going over the "Husband Manual." It's like they are in a book club. They talk about what chapter they are reading and what is working and what isn't.

Mrs. Johnston was talking about muttering under her breath, and she was giving demonstrations. "I like to tell him something just when he steps in the shower," she said, "and all he can hear is my voice with his name attached."

The women all laughed, but stopped as soon as I came into the room. As quick as a cat, Mrs. Johnston changed the subject to hot flashes.

That's in Chapter 22 of the "Husband Manual."

— November 9, 2003

90

*Eric, Tim, Barrett and Molly at their parents' renewal-of-vows,
1990*

Beware of wives bearing explanations that can make you crazy

In her ongoing effort to drive me nuts, the Truly Unpleasant Mrs.
Johnston has switched to a new game plan.

Her old scheme was pretty straightforward. She'd simply do things
like tell me to go ahead and start the car because she'd "be out in just a
minute." She'd let me sit in the car for an hour or two, then finally show

91

up and explain she'd gotten tied up "telling the kids we were leaving," making a quick call and getting a coat.

But now, Mrs. Johnston has a sneakier tactic.

I figure she must know that after 25 years of being together, her husband is wise to her tricks. So she's decided to make me believe I am just a plain, old-fashioned nut and she is not the one driving me crazy.

(I recommend that all newly married men take careful notes because it won't be long before their blushing brides are invited to the underground club that all wives join to learn the secret handshake and get the handbook called "Driving Your Husband Nuts.")

This is how she is doing it:

Let's say we are watching television and I have to leave the room for a moment. Maybe to make a sandwich or visit the bathroom. When I return, I immediately notice something is wrong.

Instead of cops chasing people through the streets with guns blazing or young women trying out for the National Bikini Wax Contest, there is a show about how to fix radishes for a dozen different special occasions. There is an earnest woman in an apron carving a radish so it looks like Abe Lincoln.

"... and this will complete your centerpiece for your annual Presidents Day celebration," the cheerful woman is saying as she places the bearded radish next to the one that looks like George Washington.

"Weren't we just watching 'Law and Order: Shoplifters Gone Bad'?" I ask Mrs. Johnston.

"Ha!" Mrs. Johnston chuckles. "That's over. Remember? They arrested that guy for trying to steal the burrito from the 7-Eleven. Then you said you wanted to watch the show on the Vegetable Display Channel on how different cultures celebrate Presidents Day."

"I did?" I say.

"I swear," Mrs. Johnston clucks in that motherly tone she uses on the kids, me and the family dog. "You would forget your head if it wasn't screwed on. You said when you saw that ad for the Vegetable Display Channel that you wanted to see how to make radishes into presidents."

"I did?" I said.

"Yes," Mrs. Johnston said, thinking that she had me on the ropes. "You also said you wanted to watch Martha Stewart talk about the plate patterns she was taking to prison."

"I did?" I said, suddenly feeling very sleepy as I heard the Radish Lady's voice quietly droning on in the background about the joys of radish sculpting.

"Don't you remember? It was right after you watched the show on making paper doilies out of wet maple leaves pressed between the pages of the phone directory," she said. "You said it would be fun to have the kids work on them with you."

I started to say, "I did?" when I snapped back to reality. It was something in what Mrs. Johnston had just said that was like a cold slap across my face.

"Did you say I thought the kids would like to work on doilies with me?" I said. "Ha! Now I know that you're messing with my mind. The only thing the kids would ever press between the pages of a phone directory would be a brother's face."

I could tell Mrs. Johnston knew she had been caught in her attempt to drive me nuts. But she just smiled, and I got the creepy feeling she was going over different ways to accomplish her goal.

The best way to keep myself sane, I decided, would be to stop listening to Mrs. Johnston completely. That should work.

– September 19, 2004

Think you're quitting to strike it rich? Not so fast, pal

After the Truly Unpleasant Mrs. Johnston read in the Aug. 22 Sunday Punch that her beloved husband was planning to quit the column-writing business and start doing something to make him a millionaire, she walked over to me and gave me a "love tap" on the back of my head.

After picking myself off the floor and rubbing the back of my head where the "love tap" left a knot the size of a walnut, I managed to say something like, "Wwwwhhhaaattt??"

Taking that sound for a question, Mrs. Johnston waved the offending column in front of my face. She had Pacific Northwest magazine rolled up and was swatting me with it like I was a dog who had torn up her garden. It became clear to me that for some reason the thought of me quitting the column-writing business and going into business for myself upset Mrs. Johnston

In the offending column, I said I had made my living for the last 35 years as a writer. But when someone tells me that they are a "freelance writer," I usually say, "So you don't have a job?" Next to saying you are a poet, the least likely job description to bring food to the table is calling yourself a freelancer. Fortunately for me, I have always been able to do my writing for newspapers. In other words, I had a steady paycheck with benefits.

Some of my friends have made money as freelance writers, but they were able to write a book and get a movie deal. Most of us scribes toil away at keyboards, putting out thousands of words over a lifetime, and then retire with cardboard boxes stuffed full of newspaper clippings. When we die, the family is left to decide what to do with thousands of those clips. In my lifetime, I have had almost 5,000 stories published with my name attached to them. Sure, some of them covered historic events — the front page of The Seattle Times on May 19, 1980 was devoted to the eruption of Mount St. Helens, and my byline was the only name on the front page. I have also written more than 300 Sunday Punches, but most of my stories were routine crime, business and government doings. Not the stuff of history.

So when I wrote the column saying I wanted to get out of the writing business and into the money-making business, it was more like a daydream than an actual plan. I see it like that Monty Python skit where they all dress up like Canadian Mounties and one of them says he always wanted to be a logger. He rips off his Mountie uniform and underneath he's wearing a flannel shirt, and he's got on logger boots. He sings a song about a lumberjack who "sleeps all night and works all day" while strutting around with an ax.

I like that part of the skit. It loses me when the logger confesses he really wants to wear dresses and a push-up bra. Of course, I didn't say *anything* like that. All I said was that my true calling was to get into business, make a million and retire to a life of leisure.

Well, I did retire, but not to a life of leisure. I don't have to punch a clock, but I still have to punch typewriter keys to write stories. Mrs. Johnston reminded me that my past attempts in business haven't proven very successful. There was a time when I thought I would become a land baron. I actually owned three houses in Seattle and rented them out. But I was a soft touch for a sob story and rented them to people who could tell great sob stories but couldn't pay the rent.

I sold the houses and got out of the land-baron business. There were other attempts at making my millions (the latest is purchasing $5 in state Lotto tickets when the prize gets over $3 million), though it looks like I'm stuck with writing — which means, fortunately or unfortunately, you are stuck with me.

But enough about my dreams. I have to get back to writing something for a buck. Mrs. Johnston is standing behind me. She has a wooden ruler in her hand.

"Don't look around," she says. "Just keep typing, buddy."

– October 1, 2006

Men, admit it: We're out of our league when it comes to arguing

A couple of researchers found that a husband could get into an argument with his wife and forget what the argument was about 15 minutes later. A wife will get into an argument with her husband and remember every little detail 15 *years* later.

When I read about this study, the only thing I could say was, "Well, duh!"

Anyone who has been married for more than a week knows that the memories of men and women are completely opposite. Men can't remember birthdays or their children's names, but they can relive every play in the final quarter of a high-school football game they were in 20 years ago. A woman may not remember her husband telling *her* about that big game he played 20 years ago, but she does remember not only his birthday but also the birthdays of his brothers and sisters as well as his parents.

When it comes to remembering arguments, wives play totally unfair. I won't say they take notes during arguments, but women seem to have an uncanny knack for remembering certain things that men forget, like details.

Basically, in arguments I like to use the 30-second rule while The Truly Unpleasant Mrs. Johnston believes in the 30-year rule.

I approach arguing with Mrs. Johnston with the idea that I still have to live with her after the argument so I want to make my point and get on with living. Thanks to a short attention span, I can usually get my point across within the limit of 30 seconds, forget what we were arguing about in the next 30 seconds and move on to another subject.

Unfortunately, Mrs. Johnston doesn't believe in the rapid-fire argument. She likes to mull over the various statements her husband made in his allotted 30 seconds and come up with a reasoned rebuttal. The reasoned rebuttal may happen right after Mrs. Johnston has heard her husband's argument. Or it may happen several days after the argument when her husband, who said his 30-second piece of pure logic and then went about his life, forgot the whole point of the discussion.

So when Mrs. Johnston starts to talk in her "reasonable" voice — that's the voice she uses on her children, husband and wild animals — about some event that rings a vague bell in the back of my head, I should be smart enough to nod in agreement and hope I'm not caught with a direct question about the old battle.

But here is where those researchers say the breakdown between men and women comes in. Women are not content to debate the general idea of the argument; they want to go over each and every point of it. Mrs. Johnston even goes so far as to remember what I said during my 30 seconds.

(I must digress here. When it comes to remembering stuff, I have to depend on Mrs. Johnston's memory. She will remind me what I said I wanted to pick up at the store and what I was going to write about. She'll tell me the story I just told someone was the same story I told that person a week before, only now it has a different ending. When it comes to details, I am at a disadvantage. If Mrs. Johnston said I said it, then I must have. I was going to say one more thing here but I forget what it was, and Mrs. Johnston isn't here to remind me, so I'll just get to the next paragraph.)

When you can't remember what you said in an argument, the other person can make up all sorts of terrible things and claim you said them. In your defense, all you can do is say, "Yeah, but . . ."

The last time Mrs. Johnston and I exchanged words and she came back with a snappy retort a week later, I promised myself I would take notes during our next argument so I can say something witty the week after.

I'll just have to ask Mrs. Johnston to remind me to get a pen and a piece of paper.

– October 12, 2002

Unmasking the feminine mystique: it's a secret society, guys!

For the past 17 years, the Truly Unpleasant Mrs. Johnston has been keeping a secret from me.

Actually I suspected she was hiding something, but I didn't figure it out until just recently. Mrs. Johnston, it turns out, is a card-carrying member of MUMS (Mothers' Underground Mutual Supporters). They even have their own national holiday: Mother's Day.

Like most males, I had no idea that an organization like MUMS existed, but I always suspected there was something going on.

Now that I know about MUMS, a lot of mysteries started to make sense. I remember the first time I noticed the secret society that I realized was part of MUMS.

When I was in high school, I was walking down Colby Avenue in Everett with a female student. As we walked by other women, the female student would smile and say "Hello" to them. The passing women would smile and say "Hello" back to her.

It was like they were old friends or maybe neighbors. Either way, it seemed that they knew each other. I thought either she was extremely popular or it just happened that everybody she ever knew was walking down Colby Avenue that day.

After we passed the fifth or sixth woman and they both exchanged pleasantries, I said that I was surprised by how many people she happened to know. That's when she told me something that later on I would connect to MUMS.

"I don't know them," she said.

Whoa! She didn't know these women, but she was smiling at them like they were long-lost friends and shouting greetings at them? When I asked her why she was doing this, she looked at me like I was the one who'd lost his mind.

"I'm just being friendly," she said.

As a male, I viewed this "being friendly" business with suspicion. I didn't realize at the time that saying "Hello" to complete strangers was part of the training women had to undergo before they joined MUMS.

If I walked down the street, smiling and saying "Hello" to every guy I happened to pass by on Colby Avenue, I would probably be popped up the side of my head before my third "Hello."

"You gettin' smart, buddy?" would be the question I would expect to receive.

But women get to join a secret organization like MUMS, an organization that men aren't allowed to know about and, if we should ever find out about it, aren't allowed to understand it. Maybe the MUMS enforcers might even kill me to make sure their secret stays safe.

Using The Truly Unpleasant Mrs. Johnston as an example, this is how I think it works: As women grow up, they are initiated into the secret society by their mothers. There is some secret code they use so they can acknowledge other members whenever they pass each other on the street.

I believe the secret signal is a smile and, "Hello. How are you today?"

They don't have a list of MUMS members. They just know who belongs, which is another scary part of the club. But being a member has some perks. They all know each other and they go into action when they become mothers.

The way I figured it out was when Mrs. Johnston left town to visit her mother (I think they call this "Returning to the mother ship") and she left her children in my care.

When I asked some basic questions about the children's care and feeding — like what time they went to school, what time was soccer practice, what they wore and what they ate — Mrs. Johnston turned to me with glassy eyes and said, "Don't worry. It's all been taken care of."

Sure enough, a backup team of MUMS just showed up at our house and everything was done.

What a great club! MUMS deserve a holiday.

– May 12, 1996

A properly doting wife can say it all with her eyes

The other day I was watching a politician on television, and while he was speaking, his devoted wife was standing next to him, watching him with absolute love in her eyes. She looked at him like he had been in a coma for 20 years and suddenly started speaking.

"I wish you looked at me like that," I said to the Truly Unpleasant Mrs. Johnston.

"What?" Mrs. Johnston said, not looking up from the book she was reading.

I mistakenly took Mrs. Johnston's "What?" as an actual question — as in, "Whatever do you mean, my beloved?" — and not her real meaning, as in, "What are you talking about? I was reading my book, and now you are bugging me."

"Do you see how that wife looks at her husband as he denies he stole money from the taxpayers?" I said. "Even though the evidence against him is overwhelming, she still looks directly at him with sheer devotion. It's like she is reading his lips."

"What?" Mrs. Johnston said again. Apparently she wasn't reading my lips with a look of sheer devotion.

"I've been noticing this gaze on the faces of wives as they watch their husbands speak, and I find it endearing," I said. "I mean, this guy is being accused of stealing money. They have videotape of him accepting gym bags full of cash from undercover agents. Everyone knows he is lying when he denies it, but his wife stands next to him and looks at him as if he is accepting the Nobel Prize."

"What?" said Mrs. Johnston, keeping up her relentless line of questioning.

"Even when the husband is accused of having affairs with different women," I observed, "you can count on the wife to be sitting at his side, gazing at him with the utter conviction that he's being honest when he says, 'I never had sex with that woman.' The husband may have been arrested for some crime, but the devoted wife will be right there during the press conference, never taking her eyes off his rolling eyeballs and his stuttering lips," I said.

"What?" Mrs. Johnston said again. She never put down her book. If this was a ploy on her part to trick me into saying something stupid, it was working.

"I've even noticed it among people who aren't married," I went on. "I was watching the news the other night, and when the male anchor was speaking, the female anchor was watching him like she never saw a person speaking full sentences before. At least not a male person. But when the female anchor spoke, the guy just glanced at her and went back to reading his script."

"What?" Mrs. Johnston said, refusing to take the bait and actually look at me.

I knew in my heart if her gaze fell upon my handsome, rugged face, she wouldn't be able to take her eyes off me and would spend the evening gazing at me. With love in her eyes and a smile playing off her lips, of course.

"Even when the woman suspects her husband is a complete moron, she still has that look," I said. "Take Laura Bush. She stands next to her husband and looks at him the whole time he is speaking. She doesn't smile, and I've never once seen her break out laughing, unless George tells one of his jokes that no one else understands.

"Maybe that is a sign of marital happiness and pure love. A wife will stand by her man no matter what. She will listen to him talk with love in her eyes, no matter what nonsense the old boy is spouting out. Don't you agree?"

I turned to look at the Truly Unpleasant Mrs. Johnston. Her head was tilted toward me and her eyes were partly closed. I thought I detected a tear in the corner of one of her eyes. She was so overcome with love and devotion, I thought, that she couldn't look directly at me.

"Don't you agree?" I gently repeated.

"Zzzzzzz," Mrs. Johnston said.

– September 21, 2003

By 2009, the Johnston children were discovering their own joys of parenting.

Remember that houseful of kids?
What happened to them all???

I have four kids.

That's how I started the first Sunday Punch column more than 15 years ago. It was written during those days when people didn't have big families or any family at all. Couples would get together to buy big houses and big cars with their big incomes. They even had a name for their breed. They were called DINKs, which stood for Double Income, No Kids.

Mrs. Johnston and I were not big into following trends. Instead we formed our own group that announced its purpose in our name. We were called SILKs. That stood for Single Income, Lots of Kids.

As I said in that first column when I told folks how many children we had, people looked at me like I had lost control of my bodily fluids. I have to admit that I did not have much control back then, but Mrs. Johnston had that situation fixed. That fix helped her earn the nickname of "The Truly Unpleasant Mrs. Johnston."

We still have four kids. But a funny thing happened in the past two decades. The "kids" have grown up and become young adults. We believe they are capable of living on their own. They know how to boil water so they can cook. They know they should bathe and change their clothes. We hope they will pay their bills and do all those things that responsible adults do.

Even if they don't do all those things, life has a way of slapping you in the back of your head and screaming, "Wake up and get with the program!" when you don't do what is expected.

Meanwhile, for the first time in 26 years, I will be alone in the family home with (drum roll, please) the Truly Unpleasant Mrs. Johnston. For the past two decades, Mrs. Johnston and I steered our lives with the kids always in mind. I think family counselors might say we were wrong, but that's what we did.

We bought a five-bedroom home because the house I was living in when we were first married was "too small." It had only three bedrooms. The same thing with the cars we drove. What happened to my car just shows people how insane I was when I married Mrs. Johnston. I owned a bright-red sports car when we met. Mrs. Johnston looked it over and condemned it with this statement:

"No room for car seats."

We moved to neighborhoods that had the best public schools, we shopped at stores where other parents like us crowded the aisles, and we ate at places that advertised specials for families. We bought our clothes at stores that had kids' departments, and we went to so many Disney movies that Mrs. Johnston and I were shocked when we saw an adult movie that had potty mouth.

Our youngest child graduated from high school two years ago, and she is off to Bellingham to finish her junior and senior years of college at Western. The other children are raised, educated and on their own.

What drove home the fact that Mrs. Johnston and I are true empty-nesters was what happened when we decided to replace Mrs. Johnston's 1993 station wagon. She started looking at other station wagons and newer minivans, just in case she might be called upon to haul a Little League team to practice.

Then it dawned on Mrs. Johnston while going over the merits of a six-passenger station wagon that she would not have to haul anyone ever again, unless it was grandchildren (none so far) or her monthly book club in search of ice cream. She dropped the station wagon idea like it was a soiled diaper and bought the car she wanted.

It was the first time in more than 20 years that Mrs. Johnston made a purchase with only one family member in mind: Mrs. Johnston. She bought a brand new 2005 VW convertible. And it is baby blue, her favorite color.

She can now be seen cruising the streets of Seattle, top down, radio blasting, talking on her cell phone. She is spending her children's inheritance.

Meanwhile, I am trying to persuade her to help me live my dream. It is a simple dream where we sell our home, buy an RV the size of a Greyhound bus and set off to see the country. Mrs. Johnston said we couldn't do that "because the children couldn't visit us."

I said they could. "We could call them from Arizona and tell them which park we're in."

– October 16, 2005

AFTERWORD

The "Truly Unpleasant" speaks

Illustration Copyright © 2010 Fred Birchman

Counterpunch: The Fairly Tolerable Mrs. Johnston sets the record straight

Editor's note: It was certainly overdue, but finally in 2001 the editors bowed to the inevitable: readers needed to hear the other side from The Truly Unpleasant.

It's about time that the editors of Pacific Northwest magazine gave me a shot at defending myself.

I'm married to Steve (I'm Not A Weasel) Johnston. That's the man who has been writing Sunday Punch for the last dozen years or so. He insists on referring to me as the Truly Unpleasant Mrs. Johnston in his column, although people who know me say I am not unpleasant at all. Most of the time they would say I'm fairly tolerable.

He once referred to me as St. Nancy, but I was not comfortable with that title. Growing up in a Catholic family, I knew that to be a saint I needed to be dead and to have performed a miracle or two. So he needed to change it.

His next choice for a new name couldn't be printed in a family newspaper, so it's The Truly Unpleasant Mrs. Johnston.

To say my husband has a tendency to bend the truth is inaccurate. He doesn't bend the truth. He twists it until even the people directly involved cannot tell fact from fiction. After awhile, they give up trying.

I've experienced this firsthand. My husband has written about how we met in San Francisco 22 years ago and how he went ga-ga over me (who can blame him, he says). But he never tells the full story.

Yes, we met in San Francisco in 1979 while he was covering a criminal trial. Yes, he did tell me we were going to get married, but it was the third time we saw each other and not on the first date like The Ever Misleading Mr. Johnston tells everyone.

OK, I said yes, but not when he first asked me. For the record, he never "asked" me to marry him. He just said we were going to get married and that was it. Then he wooed me by pretending to be a sensitive and caring guy.

He did this by courting me on The Seattle Times' expense account. This is a man who likes to go to Broadway musicals and nice restaurants (he calls them "fancy-pants joints") only if someone else picks up the tab.

When he was taking me out and telling me how much he enjoys an evening of fine dining and dancing, he had his fingers crossed behind his back. Needless to say, dining and dancing are not one of our regular nighttime activities. Mr. Twinkle Toes would rather have a root canal.

But I had to move to Seattle and marry him before I learned the whole story. By then it was too late.

I know he has written about my first reaction to his house in the past, and dismissed it by saying I thought he lived like a mole. Well, he did live like a mole, and like a mole that had only three nesting places: One nest was in the kitchen next to the sink, another was a couch in the living room with a single 60-watt bulb hanging over it, and the third place was the bedroom where undoubtedly – had I dared look – I would have found old TV-dinner trays stashed under the bed.

I knew I had my work cut out for me. The same man who could order a decent meal at a San Francisco restaurant was now showing me how to cut chuck steak. In the frying pan, no less!

Steve refers to my "icy cold stare" when looking at him after he has said or done something only an idiot would do. I like to think of it as my "sweet and loving" look – the kind every woman gives her husband when he reverts to teenage behaviors.

I suppose that Mr. Grumpy would like things to go back to his bachelor days, but where would he be without me? Mr. "I'll Eat Anything" Johnston would have exploded by now. Or, if he didn't explode, he would be buried under a pile of old newspapers, dirty laundry and TV-dinner trays. And, he wouldn't have that "sweet and loving" look staring at him every day.

– Nancy Johnston
April 1, 2001

Section II
But there's more!

The "special people," as Steve liked to call them, of The Seattle Times Eastside Bureau, ca. 1991. Back row, from left, Rod Mar, Mary Cronin, Nancy Montgomery, Steve Clutter (of The Two Steves), Pamela June Dotson, and Lou Corsaletti. Front row, Debbie Cafazzo, Steve Johnston, Bill Ristow (trying to imagine how to be the editor of this group), Mr. Zucchini, and Katherine Long.

Part I

Just Ask Johnston

Steve Johnston's humorous writing may have had its widest geographical distribution in his Sunday Punch columns, but in sheer number of columns, he was far more prolific in the sometimes sharp-tongued reader-response feature he wrote for the Eastside edition of The Seattle Times between 1991 and 2000. In those nine years, Steve wrote approximately 750 "Just Ask Johnston" columns, answering two to four questions per column – and always with his inimitable wit.

Each question began with the salutation "Hey Johnston," sort of like his editors used to holler at him across the room, and the original logo that ran at the top was so odd that during the column's second year, a reader finally asked about it. We'll let Steve take it from there, in his "Just Ask Johnston" column of July 9, 1992:

Hey Johnston: What the heck does the logo at the top of your column stand for? I keep looking at it and it doesn't make sense to me. I gotta know!

Answer: We often found ourselves wondering the same thing; we just thought it was created by those crazy Seattle Times artists after working all day in a closed office with an open bucket of airplane glue. Turns out that's not it at all.

We asked the creator – and this is the answer from Times "artist" Fred Birchman:

"The reader's question is a good one. Just what does that logo stand for!!?? Not much. Come to think of it I won't stand for much either! But seriously, I think it embodies the relationship of man to God, to the universe as interpreted by the Etruscans. The fish symbolizes fidelity to the mathematical equations as transposed on the foreheads of the children of the third Dalai Lama. The rest is Greek to me."

That's just what we thought.

"Just Ask Johnston" was funny, no doubt about it. But it was useful, too. Much of it was timely material – dealing with a specific problem in a specific place – and so it would seem out of context in a collection like this one. Instead, we are sharing a number of extracts taken from individual columns over the years, just to give you the flavor of this slightly twisted "advice" columnist.

We'll begin with one entire column, so readers can see how Steve mixed things up, and then go on with bits and pieces.

Wednesday, December 18, 1991

Hey Johnston: I've always wanted to own an island. What would it cost to buy Mercer Island?

Answer: $2,740,442,664.00.

That doesn't include the accessories. Nor does it include all those pesky people now living on the island. That's the price that the King County Assessor figures the property and buildings are worth. But if you were able to convince the Mercer Island folks to sell, you would get an island surrounded by a moat that could only be reached by bridge or boat. With any luck, one of those bridges would sink again.

To those Mercer Island residents who think $2.7 billion doesn't sound like a lot, consider that the United States government could use that money to buy three B-2 bombers. Or you could buy enough Happy

Meals to feed the entire population of China and give each person a little toy.

Hey Johnston: During the big storm last month, I saw red, white and blue lightning on the Eastside. Was it just me? Was it patriotic lightning? Drugs? What caused it?

Answer: Transformers. And not those kind you buy at the toy stores that change from a space ship to the Jolly Green Giant. Tony Mouser of North West Weather Net in Issaquah said it was a combination of downed power lines, exploding transformers and lightning going off at the same time. A power line flashes a different color when it's down than a transformer when it goes boom. Puget Power said when a power line shorts out, it makes a flash and looks like lightning. Higher the voltage, the brighter the flash.

So if a line goes down close to a power source, it has a bright flash. Further down the line, it causes a blue flash. You may have seen this happen when you stuck a butter knife into an electrical outlet.

Pretty scary, huh?

Hey Johnston: What do you consider the most important invention?

Answer: Duct tape.

Hey Johnston: Last week, you promised to tell us why some freeways had one-digit numbers (I-5) while others had three digits (I-405). Geez, my family and I can hardly wait to hear the rest of the story.

Answer: Maybe you should try getting out more. But here is the rest of the story: One- and two-digit interstate highways are through routes, for long-distance driving. Three-digit interstates that begin with even numbers are usually beltways that go around a large city (I-405, for example, from Lynnwood to Tukwila). Three digit highways beginning with odd numbers are spur routes that don't reconnect with the main freeway. They just drop off the face of the Earth (we don't have any of those).

As with everything doing with government rules, there are exceptions but this is usually the way it works. Now, get a life.

Thursday, August 13, 1992

Hey Johnston: What is the scariest thing on the Eastside?

Answer: It has to be that billboard of KIRO weatherman Harry Wappler on 520 near the Bellevue/Kirkland exit. This is a huge painting that makes Harry look like he had been attacked by killer bees. It is truly a frightening sight to see Harry waving his hand at you in your headlights on a dark and stormy night.

Hey Johnston: Why is there always water on the road on Northbound Interstate 405 about a quarter mile south of the "8" mile marker? Every day I travel that route and there is water on the road - but not coming onto the road from anywhere?

Answer: Turns out our friends at the Department of Transportation were wondering the same thing, so last weekend they went out there and dug up the spot. They thought it might be an underground spring. They didn't find a spring but they did find a busted drain pipe.

Not to bore you with details, but we had to write them down, so we'll pass them along. The pipe was broken when the state was building the HOV lane, and the joint between two pipes came apart. Saturday, the state put in a flexible drain pipe as a temporary repair. A permanent repair will be done when other work is done on that stretch of highway.

But here's the question that state folks couldn't answer:

Where did the water come from when it bubbled up? As most people know, it's been drier around here than our wit. Yet there is enough water to cause a puddle on the freeway. Makes you wonder, but not for long.

Thursday, September 24, 1992

Hey Johnston: When the city of Bellevue reworked 130th Avenue from Northup to 24th, they did their usual tearing up of the asphalt and they replaced one part with their typical incomplete patch causing quite a surface bump for cars to go over. Is there something in the contract of the city of Bellevue that says they can't hire competent engineers, contractors and inspectors so their job will be completed properly without excuses and without delays?

Answer: Yes, all city contracts have a clause that says "It shall be the duty of the city to hire incompetent engineers to complete resurfacing of city streets."

Hey Johnston: Out in the middle of the I-90 bridge on the outside of the eastbound lanes, there's a tall pole with what looks like a wingless airplane on top of it. I guess it's a wind measurer. Does that mean they think the bridge is going to blow away? Am I going to be crossing the bridge one day and suddenly find myself in Kansas?

Answer: This is a weather station, only it doesn't have a tiny little weather person inside. This little baby measures how fast the wind is blowing, from what direction, if it's raining (and how much), plus humidity and temperature. This information is sent to the operator in the Mount Baker Tunnel who decides what it all means for the average motorist crossing the bridge. If things don't look good (like the bridge is sinking), they can close it down.

There is a weather station on the Evergreen Point Bridge that does the same thing. Different types of stations are along I-405 and I-5. These measure the wind, rain and road temperature to see if they are too cold, which is helpful during a snowstorm.

Thursday, December 2, 1993

Hey Johnston: Where are the ducks this fall? I have a pond in my backyard and I'm used to ducks going in and out all year round. Last spring was the biggest group of ducks we had come through and this fall there are none. Do you know where they all are?

Answer: The state Department of Wildlife said the number of ducks in the area is down a bit, but they are still hanging around. These are local ducks. In other words, they don't go south for the winter. A couple of reasons for low numbers in your pond could be that the ducks haven't moved down to lower parts of the Eastside and the ducks around here will go where the food is available. Maybe there is a neighbor with a pond who has a better bread supply than you.

Or maybe it's like one of the yahoos we work with said: "They might be ducking him because he drove them quackers. Ha!" They don't pay us enough.

Hey Johnston: Can you answer this question for me? How would I be able to get straight A's this quarter at my school at Evergreen Junior High? Please write my name in the newspaper too, so people can see that I called and contacted you. I'm 14 and live in Redmond.

Answer: As soon as we received this question, we started a national search for the answer. We called experts in the educational field and asked them this question: How can 14-year-old Debbie get straight A's at Evergreen Junior High? We received some profound tips and advice, and wrote up the answer in a 14-page single-spaced typed paper.

We left it on the kitchen table last night so we wouldn't forget it. Unfortunately, the dog ate it.

Thursday, August 18, 1994

Hey Johnston: Who is responsible for picking up dead animals along the highways?

Answer: Whenever people ask Mr. Johnston what he would really rather be doing instead of writing a column, he always answers: "Why, picking up dead animals along the highways, of course." Next to being the guy who empties the bin at the diaper service, there is nothing more Mr. Johnston would rather do on a hot summer day than scoop up dead animals.

But this job is shared by many people. If the animal is on a state highway, the maintenance crew for the state Department of Transportation gets the job. In the county, it goes to the animal-control office, and it's the same for cities. The state Department of Fish and Wildlife is responsible for the larger wild critters.

After a few years, the somewhat eclectic logo for Steve's column apparently no longer fit The Seattle Times graphic style, which required all column logos to be photographs. That didn't stop our humorist, though, and this is the logo that ran for the remainder of Just Ask Johnston.

Tuesday, September 13, 1994

DEAR READERS: Every now and then, Mr. Johnston likes to play a joke, and he puts a misleading statement in his column to see if his vast army of readers is paying attention.

Last week, we said there has never been a movie theater in Redmond (except for Bill Gates showing home movies on a bedsheet at Microsoft).

But now, thanks to dozens and dozens of alert readers, we have been informed over and over and over again that there used to be a theater in Redmond.

Many of the callers wanted to share two things:

1. They thought Mr. Johnston was an idiot.

2. The old theater was named Cine-Mond and it showed family movies until it was taken over as a porno theater by a man named Roger Forbes in 1981.

Readers remembered when it was a family theater and the owner had couches in the front row. Some of the older Redmond residents remember "making out" on these couches while "Gone With The Wind" played on the screen.

Forbes owned a bunch of adult theaters, but he sold them in the mid-1980s, made a lot of money and we believe he moved to Hawaii.

Fortunately, no one shared with Mr. Johnston what they did on the couches when Forbes owned the theater.

Tuesday, October 18, 1994

Hey Johnston: I'm calling for my wife because she's too embarrassed. She keeps hearing that geese are not migrating, they are multiplying like crazy. Why doesn't someone start a program to feed the homeless with some of those unwanted, overweight birds? Just a thought.

Answer: Here's another thought for you. How about you and your embarrassed wife being chased around the shores of Lake Washington by an angry mob who would rather kill you than kill a goose?

There are some geese you can hunt and eat, but you need a license and hunting stamps to do it. In the cities, though, you can't hunt geese or anything else. We figure the city types are the geese you have in mind for homeless dinner tables. These geese are protected not only by law, but by a whole bunch of people who love geese.

The state wildlife folks say the cities are overpopulated with geese and other waterfowl. But people really raise a stink when the cities try to get rid of them.

Can you imagine the outcry if cities announced they were rounding up the geese to feed to homeless people? One state official, however, said they were quite tasty - "like liver."

The sound you just heard was people fainting at the very idea of eating the geese. Tell your wife that several people said it's a good idea. But like the geese, it won't fly.

Tuesday, May 16, 1995

Hey Johnston: Being one of those rich Microsoft bastards, I just moved from Bellevue to Mercer Island. Am I still officially on the Eastside? I also noticed that the Interstate 90 express-lane signs in downtown Seattle say, "Car pools, buses and Mercer Island OK." I take that to mean that if I live on Mercer Island I can take my single-occupant vehicle and use the express lanes. Cool! I'm curious as to why the special treatment exists and why, for example, people from Renton or Lynnwood don't get the same privilege on Interstate 5?

Answer: Actually, you are NOT on the Eastside, and you are NOT in Seattle. You live on Mercer Island. You are on The Rock!

There are many special privileges in store for you. For example, did you know your phone number is listed in both the Seattle and Eastside directories? Of course, you wouldn't have your phone number listed. People who need to know your number already know it.

You get to drive in the car-pool lanes to the first Mercer Island exit ALL BY YOURSELF! That's part of some sweetheart deal your city leaders cut with the state when the state wanted to rebuild I-90 through the island.

Do Renton and Lynnwood get the same treatment? Ha! Your lower lip should curl in disgust just saying the names of those cities. Nobody gets the same treatment as Mercer Island.

Finally, the best privilege is that you get to read Just Ask Johnston. Your smarty-pants friends in Seattle can't say that. (Later on, we'll show you the secret Mercer Island handshake and tell you about the free back rubs given as part of the Mercer Island Citizen Club.)

Thursday, June 22, 1995

Hey Johnston: Is it recorded anywhere whether a dog has ever been to the top of Mount Rainier? I think this question qualifies for your column.

Answer: Yes, it qualifies for this column (and what doesn't?), and no, a dog has not been to the top of Mount Rainier. Dogs aren't allowed. This is from the rangers in Ashford, Pierce County.

Hey Johnston: What about green?

Answer: Recently Mr. Johnston answered a question about rainbows, and he listed the colors of the rainbow: red, orange, yellow, blue, indigo and violet. But he left out green!

Apparently that's like leaving off Dopey when listing the Seven Dwarf Editors. Readers called to ridicule Mr. Johnston.

We got the answer from "The Handy Science Answer Book," and it left out green, too. But it's a poor workman who blames his tools, so Mr. Johnston is going away to try to make amends.

We plan to visit the ocean, and while there we will try to see the Green Flash.

The Green Flash happens when the sun is setting. Just before it dips below the horizon, the sun turns green. The red rays are hidden below the horizon, and the blue rays are scattered. Those slow-moving green rays are usually blocked by pollution, but if you sit on an ocean beach and watch the sunset you might see the Green Flash.

It's a tough assignment, but we plan to try. We shall return when we get our colors correct.

Tuesday, November 14, 1995

Hey Johnston: I'm a police officer for a traffic squad on the Eastside. I just read your answer to the question about putting the front tabs on the rear license plate and the rear tabs on the front. You're incorrect there. Actually, I stop people and cite them for this all the time.

The front tab HAS to be on the front, and the rear tab HAS to be on the rear, and they have to put the year tab in the right corner and the month tab in the left.

Yes, I'm serious! I tell people this all the time, and they get really mad when I give them a $152 ticket. It has to go where it says. I don't know how people can mess this up.

Answer: It makes Mr. Johnston rest easy knowing there is someone out there pulling over the criminal element for putting their license tabs on wrong. While Mr. Johnston never said it was OK to put the "front" tab on the rear plate, the police he spoke with said they didn't know any officers actually giving out tickets for this capital offense.

Until now, that is.

Another reader called with his solution. He said if you find you have placed the wrong tabs on your plates, just switch the plates. Front to back and back to front.

Thursday, May 16, 1996

Hey Johnston: After we eat asparagus, my family notices that there's an unusual smell when we go "number one." This is something you usually don't talk about with other families, but could you check this out?

Answer: This sounds like the kind of conversation the Johnston family also has around the dinner table. But that's appropriate, because the ability to have the asparagus smell after going to the bathroom runs in families.

People have been studying this question for years. In 1956, for example, 115 people ate asparagus and did their duty. Out of that number, 46 had the noted fragrance, and 63 didn't. Six people just couldn't tell.

It was decided the odor came from an autosomal dominant gene. These are genes that are not gender-related, so you can't say men have the odor more than women.

A professor at the University of California with a lot of time on his hands found the odor came from several S-methyl thioesters. These are compounds from a reaction of acid with sulfur-containing alcohol. They tend to smell.

In a survey at The Seattle Times' Eastside office, it was discovered that 1) all but one person had this smelly experience with asparagus, and 2) the person who didn't have the asparagus experience also CANNOT ROLL HER TONGUE like the ones with the odor! The ability to roll your tongue is another family thing.

We got most of this information from the King County Answer Line folks. They have been asked this question so many times they could reel the answer off the tops of their pointy little heads.

Thursday, June 27, 1996

Hey Johnston: We live in south Bellevue and have raccoons coming to our house every night. They hang around the back yard, eat the dog food, knock over the garbage can and make pests of themselves. Here is what we are wondering: Are raccoons dangerous? How do we get rid of them?

Answer: Raccoons look so cute that you want to feed them and maybe even do something stupid like pet one. Don't. Raccoons can be dangerous, especially if approached or cornered. Plus they can do other damage.

"They will come into your house and tear it up," warns Eve Myers of the state Department of Fish and Wildlife. "We had one raccoon do over $8,000 damage."

The Golden Rule of Raccoon Control: Don't feed them! If you have pet food out, take it in at night. Keep all other food inside and make sure your garbage can is sealed.

Myers said raccoons have long memories and will repeatedly return on the chance you forgot to take the food in. What's worse, raccoons will tell their buddies about the food source and will bring them to your house, too.

Raccoons can be discouraged by spraying the areas they frequent with white vinegar or cayenne pepper, but that may also bother your pets. And it doesn't work for all raccoons.

Myers said one sure solution is to get an animal trap and capture them. However, you shouldn't drop these animals off in the woods because urban raccoons – domesticated somewhat because of their scavenging – might not survive. Maybe that doesn't bother you, but Myers said they can spread disease to other wildlife, so you might try another way:

(Parents, cover your children's eyes and ears.)

Fill up a garbage can with water and drop the trap with the raccoon in it into the water. Yes, that will drown them! Otherwise, they will keep coming back.

OK, so what do you do with a dead raccoon? We'll deal with that in next Tuesday's column.

Hey Johnston: We all know that rats are coming up in the toilets, but my husband says he heard snakes and possums are coming up, too. A joke, right?

Answer: We suppose anything is possible when it comes to popping up in your toilet. But this sounds like something your husband is telling you to get even for all those years of yelling: "Put down the toilet seat!"

We couldn't find anyone who had firsthand knowledge of a snake or possum coming up a toilet. Eve Myers of the wildlife department (see above question) said such creatures might get in your sewer after a flood, but they would be dead by the time they showed their faces in your bowl.

We don't know if that makes you feel any more comfortable when you visit the bathroom in the middle of the night.

By the way, possums, or opossums, aren't native to the Northwest. They were imported from the South during the Depression. There were Southern guys working on federal projects here who liked to eat possum. So, they brought them from their home states.

When World War II broke out, the Southern guys packed up their gear and went to war. But they left behind their possums.

Tuesday, July 2, 1996

Hey Johnston: Your column is despicable. It's terrible to drown an animal just because it's searching for food where you happen to live.

Hey Johnston: I'd like to get you fired from The Seattle Times. We know it's legal, but it's cruel and unusual punishment to drown an animal. There is a big group of us who are going to call your boss.

Answer: Oh my, this is a sample of the calls we received after Thursday's column on how to deal with marauding raccoons. A spokeswoman for the state Department of Fish and Wildlife told us that if the raccoons can't be chased away by spraying white vinegar or cayenne pepper around the areas they frequent, then they can be trapped and drowned in a water-filled garbage can.

The wildlife expert said urban raccoons shouldn't be released in the wild, away from their home territory, because they may carry diseases that could harm other wildlife.

Mr. Johnston has raccoons coming through his yard, and the last thing he would do is trap and drown one. Besides, Mrs. Johnston and all those Johnston children would not allow it.

We moved our dog and cat food inside, but the raccoons are still coming around. Raccoon experts said raccoons have long memories and don't forget where they once got a free meal.

Several readers agreed with the wildlife department's recommendation about getting rid of raccoons. One reader also sent in a humane solution. He filled his wife's pantyhose with mothballs and hung them in different spots where the raccoons like to wander.

He said this took care of the problem, but we wonder what his neighbors thought of mothball-filled pantyhose hanging off his house.

Tuesday, October 15, 1996

Hey Johnston: I see three new comics debuted in The Seattle Times. The comics aren't very good, but that's not the point. How come readers weren't asked what comics they would like to see? I'm one of the people who responded to The Times' comics survey a couple of months ago, and I'm peeved that nothing has been done with the survey results. What gives? Don't you guys . . . (blah, blah, blah).

Answer: We hate to interrupt your tirade against Mr. Johnston's beloved employer, but we believe we had got your point by the time the spittle started running down your chin.

Mr. Johnston was also surprised to find someone had fooled with the comics. At the risk of sounding like he is sucking up to The Times' Powers That Be, he thinks the newspaper's comics are the best around and doesn't like people messing with them.

We put your question to The Times' comix czarina, Pat Foote, who said that the paper did ask for the readers' opinions and that the three comics removed – "Kidspot," "Fusco Brothers" and "Committed" – had scored the lowest.

Ms. Foote said the three replacement comics – "Tommy," "Second Chances" and "PC and Pixel" – are being taken for a test drive.

Only a few people have called about the replacements, Ms. Foote said, and most of those callers agree with you about the new strips.

"The comics are serious business, Mr. Johnston," said Ms. Foote as she ended her lecture. "If you could draw like Gary Larson, you would be rich and retire. Instead you are still writing your cheesy column."

Wednesday, June 17, 1998

Hey Johnston: When my neighbor places his recycling and garbage bins on the street for pickup on Fridays, he tends to leave them out all weekend. When he finally brings them in, he leaves it all piled up in front of his garage where it's unsightly and makes our neighborhood look bad. Isn't there an ordinance against this sort of thing? You'd think he'd figure it out on his own out of common decency, wouldn't you?

Answer: Maybe this neighbor's parents didn't raise him right, or maybe he is like Mr. Johnston, who tells his children one of their responsibilities is to bring in the garbage can and recycling bins. Then the cans sit by the curb for a few days while the children point at each other and say, "I did it last time!"

Unfortunately, there is no law requiring your neighbor to put his recycling bins and garbage can behind his house or in the garage, says the gentleman who handles recycling in Bellevue. As long as they aren't in the street, they can become part of the neighborhood scenery.

How about doing something radical and talking to your neighbor? Or drop off a note, gently suggesting that it would improve the neighborhood appearance if there weren't recycling bins on the street.

Part 2

The Two Steves

In the early to mid-1990s, the Eastside Bureau of The Seattle Times – "The Special Bureau," as Steve Johnston fondly called it – was apparently so far out of control that someone had the bright idea of having him write restaurant reviews, along with the butt of his frequent in-office jokes, Steve Clutter.

Thus was born "The Two Steves."

In all, this fearsome pair wrote a dozen or so of these little gems. We are sharing a few of them just to give you an idea of the utter chaos that could sometimes result. (These columns are slightly edited to remove outdated material about prices, etc.; rest assured, the "humor" has not been touched.)

June 10, 1994: Toy's Cafe, Bellevue

My ever-observant colleague Steve Johnston burst into the newsroom the other day and announced that he'd found a new restaurant for us to review – a place called Toy's Cafe in Old Bellevue.

Some new joint. Turns out Toy's Cafe has been in Bellevue since 1945, making it only a few years older than Johnston, and nearly as old as his jokes. My first clue about it being so old was the Arden Dairy clock on the wall. And Johnston, who grew up around here, actually remembered drinking Arden milk.

"If I was a good boy, I got cookies with my Arden milk," he explained.

"What kind of cookies?" I asked.

"Well, come to think of it, I don't know," he replied. "I never got any."

This was an upsetting revelation to Johnston but, fortunately, our waitress showed up to take our orders. Two of our fellow staffers, Pamela June Dotson and Lou "Iron Belly" Corsaletti, were dining with us. Lou wanted something "real spicy," so the waitress suggested the Mongolian beef. I had the same, but requested the "medium hot" variety. The tasty entrees were served with a large bowl of white rice and won ton soup.

Johnston will tell you about the lunch specials he and Pam ordered.

If any Chinese restaurant can be called a "meat-and-potatoes" place, it would have to be Toy's. While our two dining companions, Lou and Steve (My Lips Move When I Read) Clutter ordered from the menu, Pamela June and myself went for two of the four combination lunch plates. They all came with egg fu young soup, pork-fried rice, tea and fortune cookies. Pamela June, like a good first date, selected the least expensive plate, which came with all of the above plus a main dish of sweet and sour pork while I picked Combination C, which came with almond chicken and the rice and other goodies.

Toy's is a very small restaurant with a small kitchen, but it has a large menu ranging from appetizers to chow mein to sweet and sour dishes. When I suggested we start off the lunch with barbecued pork, Clutter said he wanted "pot stickers." But when they arrived at the table, I could tell by Clutter's wrinkled brow that he was confused.

"These don't stick to nothing," he said, picking up a pot sticker and trying to paste it to his forehead. "The stickers I get in my Happy Meal at least stick to my head."

We had to gently explain to him that although the restaurant is named "Toy's," it doesn't mean they sell toys. I didn't ask Clutter what he thought "chow yuk" might be.

I already know. It means eating with Johnston. Summing up Toy's Cafe is simple. It met the three basic requirements of a Two Steves' restaurant: The food was hot, fairly cheap and didn't take long getting to the table.

Summing up Clutter is even simpler: The mind was blank, the conversation idiotic and it didn't take long for him to gulp down a few pot stickers. But I have to agree with him that Toy's is a Two Steves kind of place. A meat-and-potatoes Chinese restaurant.

February 11, 1993: Piecora's Pizza, Kirkland

Whenever the Two Steves go on a restaurant review, we like to find a restaurant that presents a challenge. The challenge can be either trying to find the place or just eating the food. So when we heard that Piecora's in Kirkland had lost its power, heat and lights – and was having a hard time cooking – because of the Inaugural Day storm, we couldn't wait to get there.

Piecora's likes to say it has "the original New York pizza" and my dining partner, Steve ("That's MISTER Stupid To You!") Clutter, said he wanted to go there to see it in person. "The original pizza must be pretty old by now," he said.

I wanted to go there to see if they could cook a New York pizza without any heat. Just in case, we brought along fellow reporter Scott Williams, who claimed he visited New York once and ate a pizza while there.

As it turned out, Williams was confused; he had actually visited New Delhi, where he had eaten something that sounded like pizza but was made out of rice.

Regardless, we went to Piecora's where they were, in fact, still cooking. Not with electricity, but they still had gas.

The menu was limited because there were no lights or heat, but they were serving pizza and salads. We started with the Sweet Italian which normally comes with sweet fried peppers, fresh garlic and Italian sausage.

The owner, who is coincidentally named Dan Piecora, said they couldn't serve sausage because the electricity was off, sidelining the refrigerator, so they subbed Canadian bacon. I'll let my dining partner tell how it tasted.

As my culinary chum mentioned, we began our eating adventure with the Sweet Italian. We had to order another pizza, though, because several of our office mates had tagged along. For our second selection, we got a half of a Brooklyn, which has pepperoni, mushrooms and black olives.

That really made Scotty excited. He even showed us how they eat pizza in New York. He folded over the crust and stomped on it.

"It's sort of like a sandwich," Scotty noted.

Mr. Piecora reached for the phone. I think he was calling 911.

Then Scotty quit chewing long enough to blurt out something about it being the best pizza he'd ever had.

Mr. Piecora put down the phone.

I think my reviewing partner would agree with Scotty's assessment. This is not the sort of pizza you get from the chains. It was unique and delicious and Scotty, who was gnawing on crust like a dog on a bone, couldn't get enough. In fact, he threatened to punch anyone who reached for the last piece. My dining partner, who was up at the counter asking if they gave away balloons, didn't hear Scotty's threat. When Johnston sat down, I pointed at the pan. "Last piece is yours, pal."

It's one of the meanest things I've ever done and I'm sorry.

Not as sorry as I was for agreeing to have lunch with Clutter and those other unpleasant people. Plus I was even sorrier that we couldn't try the full menu which runs from pizza to heroes to soup & salad or the slice and salad. Plus a full menu of pastas and salads.

Of course, to try more items on the menu would mean spending more time listening to Clutter tell about his collection of fleas dressed up in formal wear.

March 26, 1992: Brief Encounter, Bellevue

Recently some of our more alert readers pointed out that several of the Two Steves restaurant reviews – while amusing, juvenile and sophomoric – lacked a necessary review ingredient: There was no information about the food and what it tasted like. Or even if it was served.

We will correct that oversight for our review of Bellevue's Brief Encounter. We had lunch there the other day and the regular customers won't like to hear this, but the food was great, the service was good and the price was right.

Reason the regular customers won't want to hear that is because the Brief Encounter is almost as small as the brain pan of my dining partner, Steve Clutter. As you can tell, we have finished talking about the restaurant and are now moving on to being sophomoric and juvenile once again.

As my dining partner mentioned, the food was really good. The menu is filled with tempting items with eight varieties of hamburgers and 11 other hot sandwiches, including hot beef and hot turkey.

I had the chicken fillet special, which featured breast of chicken covered with a rich mushroom gravy. Mashed potatoes and salad came with the meal, and the mashed potatoes were real, not the box variety. My observation of that fact during the meal prompted Johnston to wonder if it was harder to grow instant potatoes as opposed to real potatoes.

"Only at harvest time," I explained.

"Creamed corn must be really hard," says Johnston.

I was happy when the waitress brought him his food.

I had the patty-melt with a cup of beef vegetable soup. It was served by Chris, who is the daughter of the owner, Darlene. This is the kind of place where everyone knows each other and you can rub elbows with some elected officials (if you actually want to rub anything with them). The soup came with a generous piece of beef and the patty-melt with a thick slice of white cheese.

As most people on the Eastside know by now, my dining partner Steve ("I Don't Need No Helmet") Clutter recently broke his collarbone playing football with guys half his age. Watching him handle a knife and fork is even more amusing now that he looks like a giant bird with a bad wing. Luckily for me, Clutter didn't ask me to cut up his chicken fillet. He worked it over pretty good with his spoon and then he nailed my hand with the fork when I tried to snatch a bite of it.

This is a friendly place that is crowded for lunch and then crowded most of the rest of the day. There are eight stools and six booths. The cafe is decorated like it stood still in the 1950s. Customers bus their dishes if they want and serve coffee if Chris is too busy. When asked what time the place opens, Chris asked: "What time do you get up?" Apparently her mother comes in at 3 a.m. to get things started and the Bellevue police stop by for a cup of coffee.

Although Clutter and I usually write equally in this review (for example I write two sections and he writes two sections), I do believe my dining partner has lost count, because he's disappeared. But I can wind this baby up by saying we had two pieces of homemade pie for dessert. I had banana cream pie that was as light as a Clutter thought, and Clutter had a piece of raspberry pie with ice cream.

I'm back now. I forgot the first rule of business around here is never to leave a story open on the computer when Johnston's around. He forgot to tell you the pie is good enough to make my Midwest mother jealous. Johnston got a bit upset when my pie came, though.

"My friend didn't order ice cream," he shouted. "He asked for 'a la mode' on it!" I told him I'd eat it anyway.

About the Author

Steve Johnston has been a journalist for more than 30 years. He retired from The Seattle Times after 26 years working as a reporter, editor and columnist. His most popular columns were Sunday Punch, which ran in Pacific (later Pacific Northwest) magazine, and the Just Ask Johnston columns.

He has also been happily married for more than 30 years to the Truly Unpleasant Mrs. Johnston and has four lovely children, three grandchildren and a dog.

5716922R0

Made in the USA
Lexington, KY
08 June 2010